MW00575215

"There will come a time, in the distant future, when the Ocean will break its chains and a vast land will be revealed to men when a bold mariner . . . discovers a new world."
Seneca, *Medea*

To Jacqueline Lenoir, Mother.

To Marie-Pascale Chevance-Bertin,
without whom I would not have discovered America.

© 2002 Assouline Publishing, Inc.

Assouline Publishing, Inc.
601 West 26th Street
18th Floor
New York, NY 10001
USA
Tel: 212 989-6810 Fax: 212 647-0005

www. assouline.com

ISBN: 2 84323 335 6

Color separation: Gravor (Switzerland)
Printing: EBS (Italy)

Translated by Jennie Chiang and Chrisoula Petridis

Copyedited by Margaret Burnham

All rights reserved.
No part of this publication may be reproduced,
stored in a retrieval system, or transmitted in any
form or by any means, electronic, mechanical,
photocopying, recording, or otherwise,
without prior consent from the publisher.

Cover: Frida Kahlo © Nickolas Maray/International
Museum of Photography/George Eastman House.
Back cover: © Pedro Violle.

FABIENNE ROUSSO-LENOIR

AMERICA LATINA

ASSOULINE

CONTENTS

FOREWORD

It all started when, as an adolescent, I came across a book entitled *The Art of the Conquistadors*. My first impression of Latin America was one of black and white—harsh white, scorched by too much sun, against the coal black of embers. It was like a vision of a wild horse coming out of the night from a forgotten dream, its legs seeming to float in the shade beneath a stone archway, pausing on the threshold from a light so strong that it could have been dissolved by it. It was a horse of a dream: the dream of America. At that moment, I made a secret vow, like the schoolboys in Valéry Larbaud's book *Fermina Marquez* who said, "Later, when we are men, we will go to South America." It was, without doubt, a vow to go see those places "whose names tattoo the skin with dreams," as the writer Alain Gerber put it so well.

A souvenir of "over there," this book is to be opened like a travel album pieced together in earlier times by those other than myself from whom I have picked up the traces. It is to be looked at as a series of images brought together in a collage that, while not a description, reveals to the reader certain meanings and connections. It is to be discovered like a treasure trove from which flow sparkling fragments of illusions enveloped in the morsels of reality.

It is a land sown with dreams and plowed with nightmares. It shelters the imaginary horizons of the explorers—seekers of routes and spices who believed they had found Paradise; of conquerers thirsting for gold and redemption who believed they had reached El Dorado; of missionaries zealous about Christ, consecrating death in order to reap souls; of "Indians" who thought they had recognized their gods, but instead had discovered their torturers; and bloodthirsty, grotesque *caudillos*—executioners operating by a sort of Grand Guignol oligarchy—and liberators arising from the depths of an ever rebellious people, gauchos drunk with freedom and immigrants sick with nostalgia, visionaries, shamans, musicians and dancers given over to the whims of spirits led astray in the labyrinth of mixed cultures. "What is the history of Latin America if not the chronicle of a marvelous reality?" asked Alejo Carpentier. How could it be otherwise, when the real America is coupled with a mythical America and, everywhere, legends cloud the issues, throwing one off track? With the inclusion of prodigious Latin - American writers serving to carry out reconnaissance, this work takes up some of these themes. Far from being a global panorama—proceeding by incisions, sampling and cross sections, in the anatomical or geological sense of the term—it tends rather to reveal an interior vision of the Latin continent, pointing out landmarks, wishing to impart to the reader a desire to pursue the deeper currents. "The joy of understanding, which is greater than that of imagining or feeling!" as Jorge Luis Borges wrote.

"For the Europeans, Latin America is a man with a moustache, a guitar, and a revolver," wrote Gabriel García Marquez. If this book manages to shake up this pitifully simplistic image, it will not have been written in vain. Following the example of the great Spanish chronicler Pedro Cieza de Leon, "I place my honor in the hands of the reader!"

Opposite:
Bolivia, Lake Titicaca, 2001.
Tinted photograph,
Roland Paiva.

CHAPTER I

TERRA INCOGNITA

Can one begin to imagine how the explorers started out? The only possible comparison is perhaps that of traveling to the moon, and yet, even in that case, the astronauts knew where they were going. The world was not yet completely round or, rather, the subject was still being discussed. Between the Middle Ages and the Renaissance, the world was vague, fluid. The first globe, that of Master Benahim of Nuremberg, didn't appear until 1492, the year of the discovery of America. For the church fathers, led by Saint Augustine, the earth was shaped like the tabernacle and, although it gradually assumed the form of a wheel or a sphere, it comprised three parts corresponding to the three sons of Noah and representing the Holy Trinity: Europe, Africa and Asia. This vast Asia, whether it be called India or Ethiopia, stretched without defined limits to northern Africa and beyond to Cathay and Cipango, China and Japan. Jerusalem was the center of this world, crossed by three rivers and surrounded by the ocean—a mystical image of the universe, where the spiritual and temporal worlds overlapped because they reflected each other.

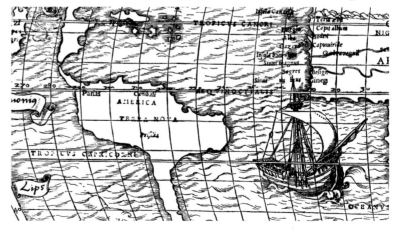

Top:
Allegory of the dominations
and lands of Holy Roman
Emperor Charles V,
and Christopher Columbus
discovering America (detail).
Painting
by Cesare dell' Acqua,
19th century.

Bottom:
In 1492, America did not yet
figure on the globe of the
cosmographer Martin
Benlaim. "Our world has just
discovered another,"
Montaigne noted simply in
his Essays *a century later.*

The way of drawing the world was still modeled on Christian dogma, but was already beginning to be altered from one map to the next, depending on the observations of voyagers and the theories of the ancient Greeks and Romans that the translations of Ficino, Chrysoloras, Petrarch and Boccaccio were bringing out of the medieval haze. Created by men who were painters as much as cartographers, these superb 15th- and 16th-century maps of the world, which were never identical—flat maps, not to be confused with globes or *portolanos*, regional maritime guides that were much more precious and used for coastal navigation—are the reflection of the questioning by the first humanists of the coded universe of medieval Christianity. The Gothic world struggled ferociously to hold back the amazing developments that were turning it upside down. From the mouths of its preachers spouted the flames of the pyres where books, paintings and heretics that dared to quench their thirst for knowledge at the sources of pagan antiquity and measure their faith at the stake of scientific truth were burned together.

Renaissance Europe was able to discover the "new" world because, underneath the Roman ruins and Greek calligraphy, it had first found the ancients. It was in the past that it would find the dynamic necessary to launch itself into the future, and it is in this double movement that lies the discovery of America, that is to say, the exploration of the Indies. This was also the moment in which the West changed from being a mystical, rigid, closed and flat world to a multidimensional space embracing both the historical and pictorial perspective. But, as well as its rationality, antiquity revealed its myths, which, even when viewed through the prism of Catholicism, supported its convictions.

In the Middle Ages faith and its symbolism were part of life; for humanity at this time, allegory had an indisputable and therefore real, if not always palpable, existence. The Renaissance Christian still shared this sensibility, even though he was no longer content simply to believe but, bringing forth the knowledge hitherto immured in the cloisters, claimed to find the verification and interpretation of the Scriptures through the study of the world. Although, until then, only the Bible had led science astray, the knowledge of the ancients as well as their myths were to nourish the spirit and the imagination of the discoverers of the Renaissance, shaping their new vision of the world.

Through the reading of Eratosthenus, Hipparque of Rhodes, and Ptolemy—whose *Geography* was the subject of a publication printed as far back as 1468—there appeared suddenly mathematical, astronomical and geographical calculations, and descriptions of physiognomy were used to shed light on researchers' intuitions. It is necessary to remember that, in Antiquity, as in the Renaissance and up until the Industrial Revolution, the sciences had not yet undergone modern compartmentalization, and no discipline was practiced in isolation. Geography and history were languages of the world, as were mathematics and philosophy, and these languages communicated amongst each other and enriched each other. The books of the Greek historian-travelers—transmitted directly like Herodotus' *Histories* or the accounts of

Ctésias of Cnidus, or compiled by others, like those of Megasthenes by Diodorus of Sicily in his *Bibliotheca Historica*—gave undreamt-of information on Persia and the Indies. But exactitude and mythology were inextricably mixed, and the question did not arise from distinguishing the fabulous from the authentic at a time when so many real phenomena were as yet unrecognized. To the readings of the Greeks were added those of the Latin authors, such as the *Geography* of Strabonn or the *Natural History* of Pliny, who traveled in Europe but never went to the Indies. The *Natural History*, which enjoyed huge authority and inspired in its turn other authors of the Late Middle Ages and the Renaissance, was a compilation of the knowledge of the Roman Empire of the 1st century. Apart from the natural sciences, zoology and botany, it encompassed astronomy, physics, geography, agriculture, trade, medicine, art and the history of nations. Translated, reworked and revisited by Christian humanism, this scholarly literature, in which myths informed the world as much as scientific observation, served to develop treatises such as those of the Bishop of Seville, saint Isadore. A type of medieval encyclopedia, the influence of its etymology, drafted in the 7th century, would last a long time—we know it was the subject of a printed edition as early as 1472.

The accounts of the voyagers who, since the 12th century, had traveled across the Far East—monks sent as ambassadors to the court of Ghengis Khan, sailors and merchants—were translated into numerous languages and widely distributed, such as the *Travels* of Marco Polo (1298), the *Travels* of Sir John Mandeville, or the account of the Venetian Niccolo dei Conti from the middle of the 15th century. In this way, from author to author, each scholar borrowed from the theories of the preceding one that which best served his arguments and demonstrations, and unverified evidence was developed and modified. Passing through the hands of several transcribers before the invention of printing, they also were told orally; indeed, they were known by Columbus as well as by all those fascinated by Asia, and they left much to the imagination. Nourished by the marvelous stories that shaped their time, read or listened to in cathedral squares, markets and inns, Mandeville and Marco Polo spent many years in these totally unknown lands. It was through this prism that Marco Polo interpreted the things that he was the first European to see, and whose forms, matter, odors and tastes were unknown up until then. As much as the places he visited, and the people, animals and plants he saw, he spoke of what had been told to him through the intermediary of translators, in a common language often badly mastered. Marco Polo, who was illiterate, dictated his *Book of Wonders*. In turn, the narratives of these first travelers became jumbled together and were at their most fantastic in popular literature comprising epics, *chansons de geste* and tales of chivalry that accompanied the 16th century in the same way as the chronicles of the conquest.

Page 10:
Anonymous French map,
16th century.

Page 11:
Map printed by Grynaeus
in Basel, 1532.
Mexico,
which was conquered
11 years earlier,
was unknown
to the cartographer.
As for Cuba, its shape
is exaggerated and leads one
to believe that there
is a strait between
the island
and South America.

Below:
Portuguese portolano,
Miller atlas, 1519.

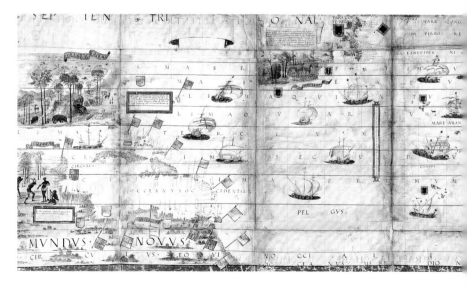

Everyone knows the story of Alexander. It retraces the fabled conquests of the great king of Macedonia who subjugated Asia and campaigned as far as India before dying at the age of 33. Through this story, Christianized versions of Greek and Latin myths blended into biblical myths. And it was following in the footsteps of Alexander the Great that the explorers—without realizing—found America, a discovery that, like a mirror struck by the sun, sent back a blazing image of the dreams and fears that haunted humanity. Ancient geography, the vehicle for a science steeped in mythology, was from then on superimposed on theological cosmography, which subjugated the representation of the real to the canons of the Church. On the maps used by Columbus, Magellan or Vespucci, figured indistinct countries at the limits of the known world—the indistinct countries traversed or described by Alexander and Marco Polo. The names became confused and their domains were exptended to infinity, following in the footsteps of the men who traveled through them, endlessly pushing back the borders of Terra Incognita. The Indies, Ethiopia, Cathay, Cipang—what does it matter? It was now a question of reaching them from the West, from the other side of the earth.

Indies or Paradise

For the 16th-century European, "legends" were what this word literally means in Latin, "things to read," whether they were found in books or in the world. For this man, as Michel Foucault summed it up in *The Order of Things*, "There is no difference between the visible marks that God has stamped upon the surface of the earth, so that we know its inner secrets, and the legible words that the Scriptures, or the sages of Antiquity, have set down in the books preserved for us by tradition. . . . Nature and the word can intertwine with one another to infinity, forming for those who can read it, one vast single text." (N.B. This quotation, the following Foucault quotation and the Paracelsus quotation are from Michel Foucault, *The Order of Things*, New York: Vintage, 1970.) The study of all these texts was, of course, reserved for scholars who attempted—by incorporating them in a single work in the image of nature—to present a mirror of the world that represented all the knowledge of their era. As Foucault saw it, "one has to collect together into one and the same form of knowledge all that has been seen and heard, all that has been recounted, either by nature or by men, by the language of the world, by tradition, or by poets." The works that comment on these books, which are that themselves compilations, do not distinguish between "observation, document and fable," all of which were considered equivalent in meaning at the time.

Overleaf, left:
Franciscan books,
16th century.
Right:
Christopher Columbus by
Ridolofo Ghirlandaio, 1519.

Exemplary in this respect is the *Ymago Mundi* drafted in 1410 by the cardinal and chancellor of the Sorbonne, Pierre d'Ailly, and printed between 1480 and 1483. Christopher Columbus' copy, extensively annotated in his own hand, provides invaluable information on the state of mind in which he undertook his voyages. In the margin, Columbus noted simply, "The Earthly Paradise is here."

For there was a time when the Earthly Paradise figured on maps from which America was missing. God had planted "a garden in Eden, in the East," and as Pierre d'Ailly, who was also known as "the Eagle of the Doctors of France" and "the Hammer of theHeretics," confirmed, some went so far as to say that "the Earthly Paradise is found on a neighboring mountain to the east." Also called the Garden of Earthly Delights, it was supposed to be located in an entirely temperate zone at the peak of a mountain high enough to have been spared by the Flood, was watered by a spring that was the source of four Biblical rivers, and planted with flowering trees that provided all that man needed without having to work for it; others added that those who lived there were eternally young. Several times, Columbus, firmly convinced that he was the messenger of God as much as the envoy of the Catholic Kings, had the impression that "The earth over there is another world," and wrote in his diary and letters "great clues" relating to the location of the Earthly Paradise. Amerigo Vespucci, who set sail after Columbus and whose first name, by trickery, was used to name the new continent, also wrote that "the trees are so beautiful and sweet that we think we are in the Earthly Paradise."

In the same way that it informed Columbus, this literature—written and oral— directed the production of maps of the worlds. Where else could representations of the earth come from? Like books, cartography is a mirror of the world as much as it is a metaphor for it. Real and mythical places both figured on maps; thus we find, beside flags and coats of arms, castles, churches and mosques, effigies of real emperors, kings and lords, the representations of kingdoms and peoples that were assumed, according to tradition, to exist somewhere, that is, in an as-yet-unexplored part of the world. The Renaissance placed man at the center of this world. In the words of Paracelsus, "There is nothing in the depths of the seas, nothing in the firmament, that man is not capable of discovering."

Beyond the Pillars of Hercules, Gibraltar's strait with its troubled waters, the unknown extends into infinity: the exterior sea, the Ocean, of which Columbus was named the Admiral. Islands there were either buoys or stumbling blocks, but always Tom Thumb pebbles on the surface of the liquid and unfathomable abyss that surrounded them. Secret islands, the bearers of all the dreams scattered on the furrows of the high seas, shifting beacons similar to the "marvelous clouds," ceaselessly pushed by cartographers to the edge of the universe, marking the end of the known world. As a result of the voyages of Mediterranean sailors and Celts, the ancients knew that islands to the west existed. Marco Polo counted 12,700 of them in the Indian Ocean, the Portuguese had already conquered the Azores and the islands of Cape Verde, and the Spanish found some of the Canary Islands. Maps and legends strew the Ocean with mysterious islands that were enchanted and enchanting, sporadic and mobile, peopled with giants, Amazons, demons, mythical birds or sirens, a fantastic archipelago handed down by Ulysses as much as by Irish sailors. While all focused their fantasies there, they were as indispensable to the navigator as feared, as seductive as dangerous.

One of Columbus' assets was a map drawn up by a very conscientious geographer and astronomer, the Florentine Paolo dal Pozzo Toscanelli. Toscanelli, who, up until his death ten years before the great departure, corresponded with Columbus, shared Marco Polo's ideas about the stretching out of Asia to the east and thought it was located only 120 degrees from Western Europe, an error that Columbus thought was the truth until the very end. Anti-ilha, which means "the island on the other side," appeared on this map. Seven bishops were said to have made a landfall there when fleeing the Arab invasion of the 7th century; each one founded his city. Portuguese sailors ran aground there over the centuries and were dazzled by the wealth and fertility of this island, where people lived in peace and where, on the shore, gold dust sparkled on the sand. Columbus thought that Antilia was near Cipango, the island that he wanted to reach, and was filled with pearls and precious stones with a "palace covered in gold plate," rooms paved with gold "thicker than two fingers . . . so rich that no one could count its wealth." Marco Polo described it thus without ever having entered it, but the subjects of Kublai Khan told him about it. Situated on the "high seas" 1,500 miles east of Cathay, Cipango was none other than "Je-pen Kouo," the land of the rising sun, which we now call Japan. Columbus never reached Cipango, which he searched for all his life, believing it to be nearby. Before leaving Cuba in 1504, during his last voyage, he named the headland east of the island, which he took for the *finis terrae* of Asia, Cape Alpha and Omega, the junction between two worlds, because, according to Saint John, God is the alpha and omega of all things. While the islands discovered by Columbus were soon known as Antillas, they are also mentioned on a map of the world from 1508, that of the Dutchman Johannes Ruych: "This island of Antilia was discovered by the Portuguese long ago, now those who seek it do not find it." As for Columbus, he is without a doubt the person whom St. John Perse called the master of stars and of navigation: "They called me the Obscure One and my subject was the sea. The year of which I speak is the greatest year; the sea that I examine is the greatest sea. . . . The earthly condition is miserable, but I have an immense possession in the seas, and my profit to the tables of overseas incalculable."

Convinced that he reached "the isles of the Indies beyond the Ganges," Columbus died in 1506, without having suspected that he had discovered a fourth continent. If it is known as America, it is again because of a cartographer's trick. Martin Waldseemüller, swayed by the arguments that Columbus' rival Amerigo developed in his letters, decided to name the New World, the fourth part of the earth, on a map that he published in 1507, after the explorer. Bowing to the reasons of Columbus' son who led the campaign to give Christopher his due, Waldseemüller revised the following edition of the map. Too late; the harm had already been done. It is fitting that this continent, discovered by chance by someone looking for a short-cut, is registered under a false name.

Opposite:
It was from the port of Cadiz
that Christopher Columbus
set sail on the Marigalante
on September 25, 1493,
his second expedition.

Overleaf, left:
Hernán Cortés
(1485-1547).
Right:
Franciscan monk
photographed in 1922.
Until recently,
missionaries still traveled
in conditions similar to
those of the conquest.

" They called me the Obscure One
and my subject was the sea. The year of which I speak
is the greatest year; the sea that I examine is the
greatest sea . . . The earthly condition is miserable,
but I have an immense possession in the seas,
and my profit to the tables of overseas incalculable. "

SAINT JOHN PERSE

Montezuma and his warriors extended their empire from sea to sea, satisfying the god's incessant hunger with the beating hearts of their captives. The blood of sacrifices and mortifications was the precious water that irrigated the universe, the liquid energy that, uniting men and gods, fed the cosmic equilibrium, the vital spring that the gods drew from the bodies of men to restore themselves day and night. Born under the sign of Quetzalcoatl, descended from the Toltecs on his mother's side, Montezuma was the priest-king who had become the faithful servant of the idol with the dragon's maw, whose seal he wore attached to his wrist. And the enemy gods had chosen him as the stake of their final combat. The life or death of his people depended on their confrontation. For ten years, terrifying omens had announced his ineluctable return. When a strange bird the color of ashes whose head was crowned with an obsidian mirror was captured on Lake Mexico, could Montezuma, the master of the Aztec empire, still have any doubts? Wasn't the "Mirror of Smoke" an attribute of Tezcalipoca through which the creator of heaven and earth absorbed and reflected the world? It was in this murky mirror that, in broad daylight, a shred of the starry night was reflected, that the god and his escort appeared, borne towards him at the rapid pace of their monstrous beasts. He had recognized it from the canvases on which his painters had faithfully reproduced the stories of his informers, who were omnipresent in his still uncertain empire.

Quetzalcoatl rose up against Huitzilopochtli, and already on his route the rebel caciques were rising and threatening the Mexicans. Cortés was there, with his long hair and black beard, surrounded by others with curly hair the color of flame or corn, fully dressed, helmeted and armed with a gray metal, mounted on tall, frothing beasts and escorted by bloodthirsty dogs—beings that no one had ever seen before, beings that, as long as thunderbolts spurted from their hands, terrorized his people—hadn't they believed that man and mount were a single creature? The much-dreaded foreigners had finally arrived from "between the clouds and the mist." "Lord, I am not asleep and am not dreaming. . . . I see you because I have already seen you." When Montezuma said these words to Cortés, was he thinking of the rite in which, borne on the back of another, a sleeping man represented the dream during the feast in which gods and men set off together to seek their destiny? Men or gods, nothing or no one could do anything about it, destiny had to be fulfilled. And Montezuma said to Cortés: "Welcome to your country, Lord: come and rest, take possession of your royal dwellings."

Cortés was 34 years old and looked like one of the portraits of hidalgos that made El Greco famous. Always dressed in black and swearing only by his own conscience, the horseman who wore a golden medallion adorned with the Madonna and John the Baptist under his beard was, according to all his contemporaries, the noblest of the conquistadors and, relatively speaking, the most disinterested. This man, to whom was attributed the cynical intelligence and the

Previous pages:
Lake, equatorial Andes.

Opposite:
The meeting of Cortez and Montezuma in Tenochtitlan in 1519. Anonymous 16th century Spanish painting. Alejo Carpentier humorously described the European paintings in which Montezuma became a figure who was "half-Roman, half-Aztec with an air of Caesar coiffed with quetzal feathers."

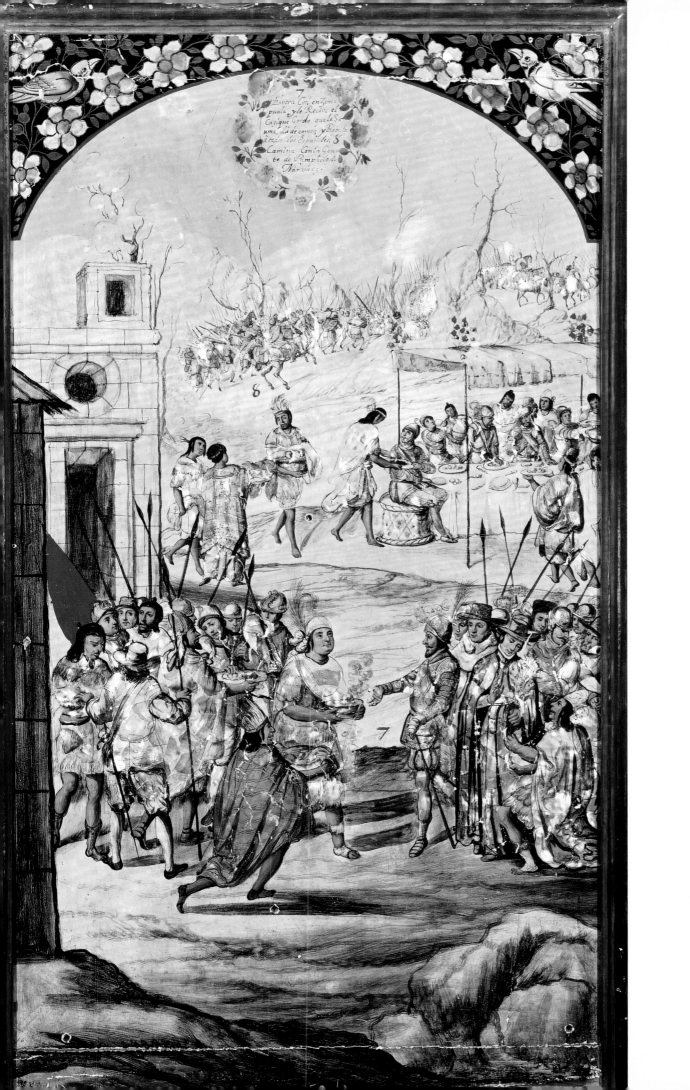

7
Entra Cortes en Zem-
puala, y le Recive el
Cazique Gordo que le Sa-
lió a comer, y Regala
a todos los Españoles. 8
Camina con la Gen-
te de Pamphilo de
Narvaez.

8

7

Opposite:
Gold coxal protector.
Albrecht Dürer, who saw
pieces of gold plate brought
back from the Indies in
Brussels, marveled "before
the subtle genius of men
from foreign countries,"
maintaining that "in my life,
I've never seen any thing that
so gladdened my heart."
(Letter, 1529)

Top:
Chimu gold crown with
zoomorphic and
anthropomorphic motifs.
Bottom:
Gold washers,
Serra Pelada, Brazil.

political genius of Machiavelli, the pride of El Cid, the wiliness of Ulysses, the bravery of Achilles and the panache and generosity of Don Quixote, possessed an unshakable will carried along by an unadulterated faith. Cortés pitted his evangelical will and his determination to conquer against Montezuma's fatalism, doubts and the faintheartedness that drove him to be the instrument of the destruction of his people. At the head of his 12 horsemen and 400 foot soldiers, who were united behind a leader whom they liked as much as respected, it was like Don Quixote, "alone and free to achieve his dream," that Cortés advanced towards Mexico City, preceded by a black velvet banner on which a red cross blazed on a ground of blue and white flames. The white city, constructed on the lake, spread its splendors out before the Spanish eyes filled with wonder. According to Bernal Díaz del Castillo, the loyal companion and chronicler of the conquest of Mexico, these coarse soldiers seeking their fortunes discovered "as if in a dream" palaces, towers, fragrant gardens, shaded terraces and quays edged with roses, "unheard of things, never seen or even dreamed . . . that resembled the enchanted dwellings in the Romance of Amadis."

Cortés razed Mexico-Tenochtitlán and brought down the Aztec idols. He offered Christ the King the sacrifice of thousands of Indian lives and to Charles V the fabulous wealth of the empire of the Indies.

The tragedy that still haunts indigenous peoples was repeated all over the continent. Deeply structured around religions whose visions and understandings of time, creation and the continuity of the world were totally alien to monotheism, Amerindian societies disintegrated at the same time that, from the top of the temples, their gods crumbled into dust. "Let us die then, let us perish then, since our gods are already dead!" replied the Aztec priests to the Franciscan missionaries who came to convert them. "Strikers of the day, offenders of the night, murderers of the world! . . . They taught fear and came to blight the flowers. . . . So that their flower may live, they damaged and sucked up the flower of others. . . . Blighted is the life and dead the heart of their flowers."

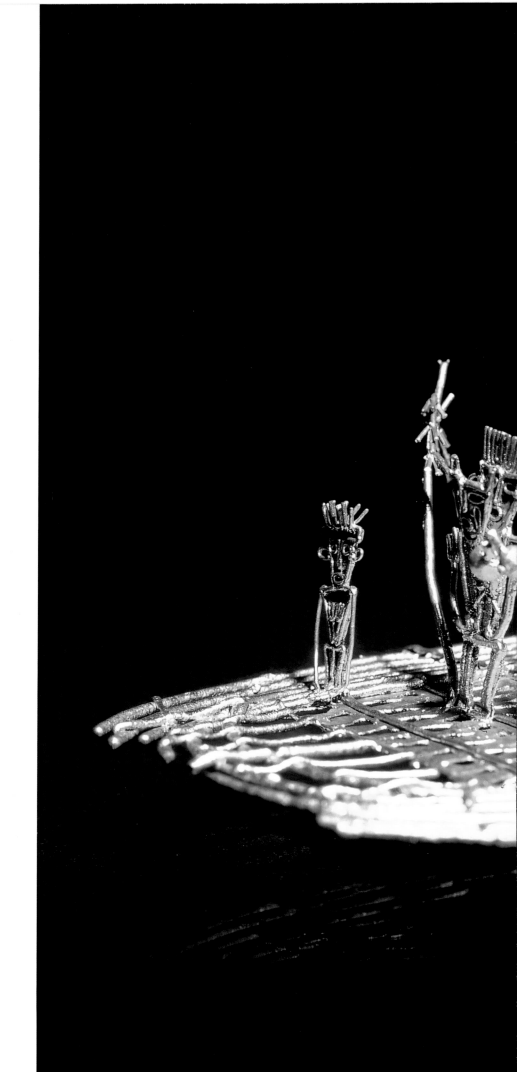

Opposite:
El Dorado, the golden king,
on his boat. Muisca votive
figurine, Gold Museum,
Bogotá, Colombia.

"Christians, if I knew that
you were going fight over my
gold, I never would have
given it to you because I am a
friend of peace and
concord. I am astonished by
your blindness and folly. You
destroy finely wrought jewels
to make bars out of them,
and although you are friends,
you fight over a thing so vile
and insignificant."
Inca testimony
about the Conquest of Peru.

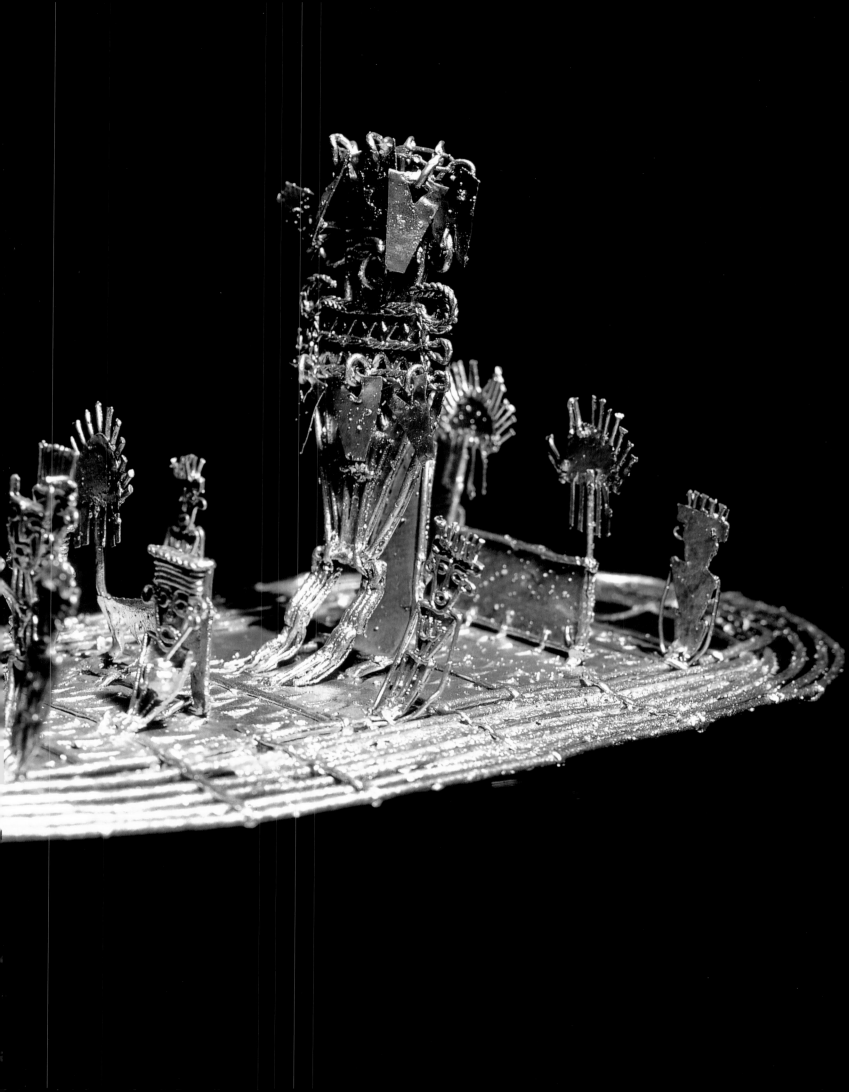

Ophir and Tarsis, the Golden Chersonese, King Solomon's Mines or the golden palace of Marco Polo's Cipango. Through the intermediary of fledgling interpreters, these are the names that the conquistadors pronounced when they questioned the Indians who, according to Oviedo, "promised the Christians what they wanted: gold," and even more so when they realized that this was the best way of sending away the invaders. Names became confused; places were superimposed on one another and moved. As gold was gradually obtained—whether it was stolen or traded for glass beads, which amounts to the same thing—more was always wanted. Columbus, who was the first, wrote to Pope Alexander VI, one of the Borgias: "This island is Tarsis, Cethia, Ophir, Ophaz and Cipango, and we have named it Hispaniola." During his fourth voyage, he affirmed that ancient Aurea, where King Solomon's Mines were found, and the beaches of Veraguas, which he had just discovered on the east cost of Panama, "were one and the same." For the attention of the Catholic Kings, Columbus added: "Solomon bought all this: gold, stone and silver, and Your Highnesses can take possession of it, if that be your will." In his wake, from the beginning of the 16th century to the end of the 18th century, over 20 expeditions were launched seeking these mythical lands, of which the discovery and conquest of Mexico (1519–1521) and, above all, Peru (1532) confirmed the existence. The hidden kingdom where the Incas who escaped Pizarro's massacre took refuge, taking with them treasures much bigger than the ransom of Atahualpa, was long sought. It was called Cíbola, Dabaibe, Paititi, Lin Lin, Trapalanda, Meta, Manoa, Lake Parime, the Land of Cinnamon or the City of the Caesars; it moved from the high plateaus of Colombia to the foothills of the Andes, from the Venezuelan plains to the Ecuadorian jungle, from the Orinoco to the Amazon. Never reaching it, thousands of men died horrible deaths. Golden Castile, Costa Rica, Puerto Rico, Rio de la Plata, Argentina, Esmeraldas: the names given to the conquered countries resonated with hope as much as with nostalgia. Although people rushed there to gather the sand that the mica made sparkle, certain that, once it was melted, it would become pure gold, Golden Castile was nothing but an insalubrious and inhospitable swamp.

But nothing calmed the fever that buzzed in the ears of the Spanish and then all Europeans. "News from Peru was so extraordinary that it carried away the old and the young even more so... There will be only one inhabitant remaining here, unless we tie them up," noted the royal officials of Puerto Rico. Oviedo noted, "They come from Italy, Germany, Scotland, England and France, among them were Hungarians, Poles, Greeks and Portuguese." What did they ask?" "Where and how one could fish for gold with nets," marveled Bartolomé de Las Casas, or rather, where it was sown and harvested! Even though many real rivers contained gold nuggets and mines really existed, those who set off for the Indies—"refuge and shelter of the helpless people of Spain, parish of conspirators and safe-conduct of murders," as Cervantes wrote in *The Jealous*

Extremaduran—dreamed, like Periander, another one of his heroes, of beaches with "sand made out of gold and pearls, fields carpeted with emeralds and rivers of diamonds."

What they found most often, which did not discourage them for all that, were mountains to climb, eddying torrents, scorching deserts and, even worse, the immense Amazonian forest. "There, there is no more light, except a diffuse brightness that warmed itself through the foliage until it became a moist, warm half-light laden with the scent of plants. . . . There, no one knew anything of the sun," wrote the Colombian writer German Arciniegas in his wonderful book on the conquistador Jiménez de Quesada, *El Caballero de El Dorado*. In the tangle of roots and trunks covered with lianas, a path was cut with a machete for men, horses and Indian slaves, beasts of burden attached to one another by a rope halter. They disappeared into the unknown, into the green labyrinth where plant life blended into animal life, trees blended into the water in the mangrove swamps and water blended into the earth, forming a spongy mud where scorpions and snakes crawled. In a day, they barely covered half a league, a little less than two kilometers, torrential rains beat down upon them suddenly, surprising men who knew nothing of the climate or the terrain. Rises in the water level made lakes appear, rapids swept along the makeshift crafts, or, on the contrary, the dry season emptied the rivers and they had to pull the brigs with a rope, taking care not to get stuck in the sediment of the muddy water. Each step was a danger, but they advanced full of fear with empty bellies, as they lacked provisions. They ate roots, horses and even dead companions. The pestilential swamps unleashed their fever-bearing mosquitoes; at night, vampire bats sucked their blood and gangrene crept into the slightest injury: in a day, a man rotted on foot. The jungle unceasingly resounded with the sound of a thousand wild sounds, which sometimes signaled Indian attacks and flights of poisoned arrows. Carrion eaters and caimans escorted the procession of knights-errant who had become shadows of themselves. Survivors were rare and returned "sick and weak, sad and defeated, in such a state that it was painful to look at them," as stated Cieza de León after returning from the expedition led in 1541 by Gonzalo Pizarro into the equatorial forest in search of the "land of cinnamon and the prince called El Dorado." "I don't think," noted Oviedo, "that many of them would have endured such fatigue in order to reach heaven itself." Later, he added, "They subordinated honor, morality and decency to reach this end and engaged in fraud, crime and innumerable atrocities." The massacres of Indians and the murders between conquistadors punctuated the search for treasure. They launched raids on villages to get fresh supplies, captured men to replace the porters dead of exhaustion, raped women, plundered tombs, tortured people in order to find out where the gold was hidden and, if they didn't find any, killed to take revenge. These expeditions followed each other, separated, lost each other, overtook each other, surpassed each other and sometimes met again;

"Who has ever held in his fist the soul of the Indians? For four centuries, they have hid their soul. Fifteen generations have affixed fifteen seals on the subterranean source of their race."

GERMAN ARCINIEGAS

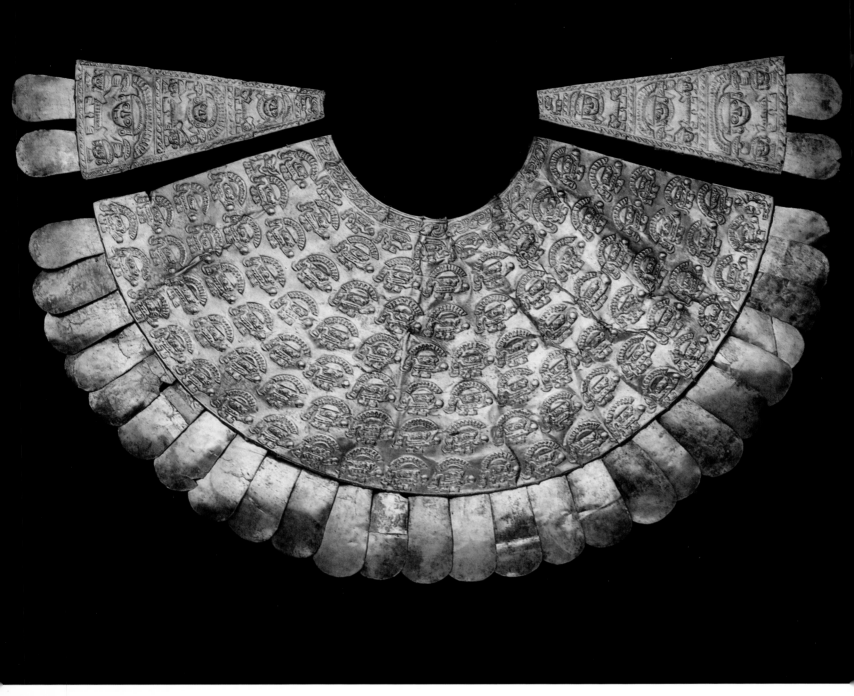

"The world was once
made of gold."

CUNA MYTHOLOGY

Conquest overflow with gold, the sacred gold that became the currency of Europe, and a few scatted scraps of which lie in the museums of the world. Words preserved by the metal, which some treasure hunters, stubborn dreamers, desperately tried to set free and which, under the gaze of the predators withdrew into itself, like the Quechua or Aymara Indians, isolated for five centuries in a silence that always surprised the voyager. In the *huacas*—mountains, trees and other recipients of divine spirits—the echo of the universe had ceased to resonate. "We closed the doors of an enchanted treasure," wrote Miguel Angel Asturias. They half open for those who, as Octavio Paz wished, knew how to "disinter the lost word." From Claude Lévi-Strauss to Gerardo Reichel-Dolmatoff, these inspired scholars watched and listened to the myths and the rites of peoples who managed to preserve their ancestral culture more than others. Where European thought did not last as long as gold—like he who only saw fire—they deciphered "the dreams of a sun dreaming of his worlds," as Octavio Paz put it so well. For "the sun created the universe with the power of his golden light," according to mythology of the Desana Indians of Amazonia. "All of this was created by the sun when he was driven by the gleaming will to create the world."

It was the goldsmith who discovered these dreams of the sun first in the dark rock in which he managed to distinguish the shiny metal. Made of the sweat and tears of the divine star, gold concentrated its creative energy. This is why it was a sacred metal: a cosmic, incorruptible, living and fertile material, an energy that could be transmitted to human beings. Reichel-Dolmatoff reports that the Indians of the Sierra Nevada de Santa Marta in Colombia—who use the same word for gold and for sun—still observe the ancient ritual of exposing gold to sunlight today. At precise dates, at a sacred site, the Indians expose to the rays of the sun their ritual objects that they managed to safeguard for 500 years; thus, they say, gold purifies itself and takes on new fertilizing powers. The reactivation of gold's energy is also an offering to the sun, which has come to feed its benign. Like blood, gold is a channel through which the dialogue between the upper world and the lower world passes. In the veins of men, blood flowed; in the sun gold, flowed. The two substances were used in the exchange between men and gods. But, like an uninitiated man, gold in its raw state remained in an uninitiated state. The master of fire, the goldsmith, was also the master of transformation. By making the metal pass various tests, various states—liquid, solid, rigid or malleable—he forged a vocabulary of metamorphosis, a vocabulary that was the shaman's responsibility to make speak. The votive objects, offerings and ornaments that the goldsmith made with his hands were messages and means of communications. Differing in workmanship and style according to the region, the era and specific beliefs, Amerindian gold objects always convey a sacred code of great complexity, of which certain keys have probably been lost forever.

Opposite:
Chimu gold pectoral
decorated with
anthropomorphic
and zoomorphic figures.

Opposite:
Gold solar mask,
Ecuador.

"The sun is a man wearing
a mask of fire"
Kogui mythology.

Below:
Four Chimu
gold trumpets.

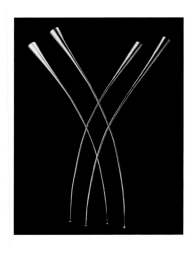

"To adorn is to adore," wrote Miguel Angel Asturias. When they affronted Aztec warriors dressed in tiger skins or wearing helmets in the shape of an eagle's head, did the conquistadors know that these horsemen had acquired the strength and the courage of the tiger, and the speed and the sharp eyes of the eagle? When they parleyed with Inca notables wearing feathered headdresses and mantles with prominent wings, with Tairona or Muiscas priests sporting pectorals sculpted into the shape of a bat-man, nose ornaments with the stylized features of a jaguar, diadems in the shape of snakes, did they know that these dignitaries possessed the qualities, senses, properties and powers of these animals? All these ornaments are masks, portals opening onto the invisible. For the initiated who wore them, they were as many doubles, new faces and other identities, which, beyond the opaqueness of the visible world, lead them towards different spheres, establishing contact with the primordial universe. Jaguar-man, bird-man, bat-man, snake-man, crocodile-man, crab-man and even man-ioc-man, corn-man and tobacco-man, these transformations could be further complicated by hybrids taking one part from each species. For the Amerindians, humans, animals and plants were filled with the same vital fluid and were part of the same cosmic balance, which comprised complementary opposites. This balance had to be respected and maintained communally in order to ensure the proper functioning of the land and the renewal of its cycles. Humans, animals and plants possessed not only the capacity to communicate with each other, but also that of joining together or "voyaging" towards each other by borrowing one or several of their specificities. Each of them could multiply their identities, become the other and thus see, feel and act in accordance with this borrowed perspective, then come back to oneself, having acquired new knowledge that would serve to better control their integration into the terrestrial world. For man, these transformations were accompanied with, under the control of the shaman, the ingestion of coca leaves and other narcotic or hallucinogenic plants that facilitated flight and the close encounter with the spirits of the mythical masters who governed each species. A solar and thus divine substance, gold, in which were encrypted the terms of the cosmic symposium, established the link between the real and mythical worlds. It is a metaphor covering with a divine veil the secret passages of metamorphosis.

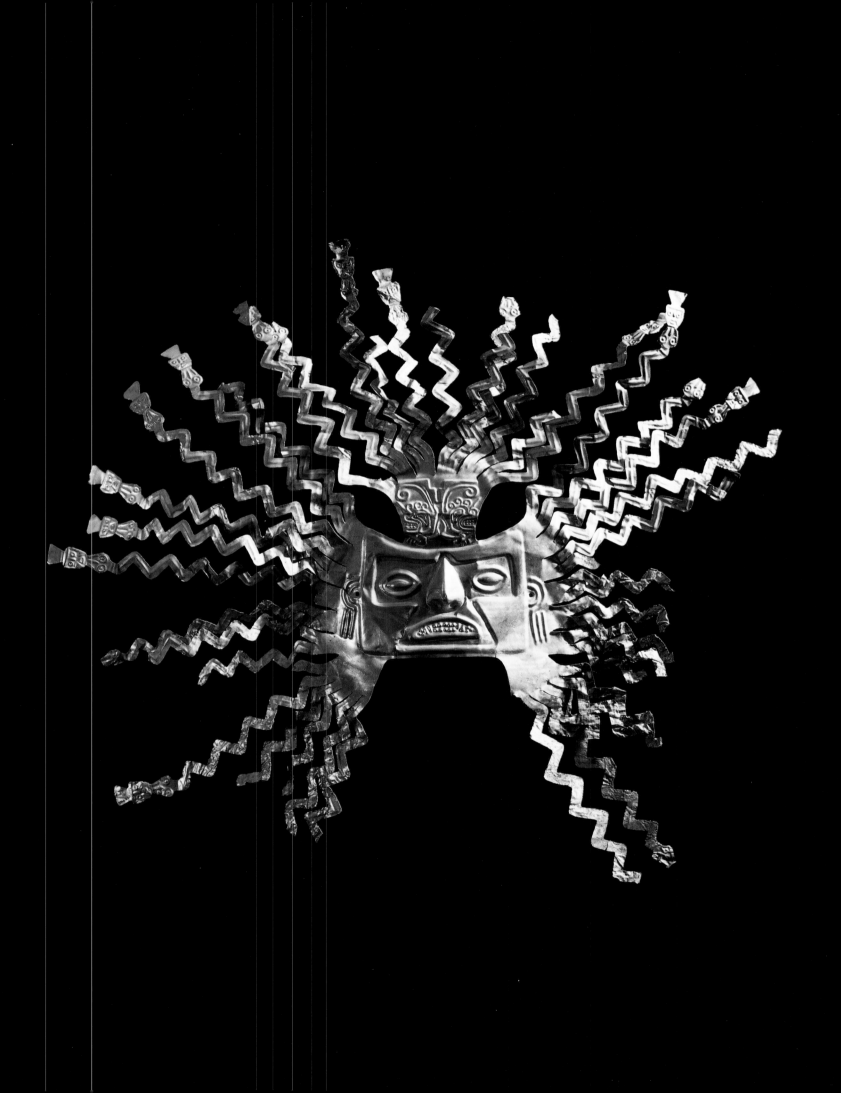

CHAPTER III

THE FORGOTTEN LANDS

Folded into the shadow of Amazonia, forgotten in the *llanos*—the plains of Venezuela or the salt flats of Atacama, sheltered in the heights of the Cordillera Blanca or the Andean lagoons, huddled against the wind of Patagonia or the roar of the cataracts, hidden away in the grass of the pampas or riverbeds, the America that existed before the conquest still holds out against the invader. In the waters of great solitude and the lands of great silence, there, the divine pulse still beats. There still awakes every morning a world of the first words and first days. There are still written what Neruda referred to as "the initials of the earth."

Llano, pampa, *sertão*, *catinga*, *arenal, pedregal, cardonal, yermo, cerro,* paramo, puna, altiplano: these words cannot be translated; only the five senses can give them meaning. Like the vermilion of the clay soil in the humid jungles, the intense cobalt blue of the Andean sky, the luminous jade of the fertile plains, Fauvist colors that Paul Gauguin alone was able to bring back from his Peruvian wanderings. Like the indigo of the Atlantic and the parrot blue of the sky off the port of Santos, as seen by Blaise Cendrars in the bay that opens out on the Tropic of Capricorn. To gaze at the white and raw clarity of the savannah, the harshness of the deserts scorched by the sun, whether they are a continuation of the sea and the rivers like the *llanos* and the *sertão* in Venezuela, Peru or Brazil, or unfurl at altitude, like the Mexican paramos and the Andean punas.

"Before the wig
and the dress coat
There were rivers,
arterial rivers:
There were
cordilleras,
jagged waves
Where the condor
and the snow seemed
immutable:
There was dampness
and dense growth,
The thunder as yet
unnamed,
The planetary
pampas."

PABLO NERUDA

It is a land of burning limestone, saltpeter and dust, cracked, crevassed, sometimes spiked with cactus, aloe or thistle plants, "where it is always midday, where the same sun falls relentlessly on a suspended landscape," as Octavio Paz said in *Llano*. "The eyes sweep across and alight on nothing," continued Juan Rulfo in *El llano en llamas* (*The Burning Plain*). The plain, "this carapace of white, hard rock where nothing moves and one seems to walk backwards." An opaque air hangs above the savannah, blurring perspective. A "still . . . empty air . . . hard and dense . . . sharp like a hot knife," said Jean-Marie Gustave Le Clézio of this Mexico that he loved so much. "Here, when one speaks, the words burn the mouth and dry out on your tongue, cutting the breath," noted Rulfo. In these isolated deserts where occasional peónes follow thirsty herds walking towards the illusory water of mirages, the suffocating dryness yields only before the roaring sound of earthy water. Then the flood comes, like a deluge, sweeping all before it, at last rendering fertile the exhausted earth, at the price of immense suffering.

The Andes

Suddenly, "the infinite horizontal metamorphosizes into the infinite vertical," wrote Alejo Carpentier. From the flat land rises up an unimaginable wall of rock, its peaks lost in the snow. But, just as Ricardo Güiraldes noted, "Describing the Cordillera would be like trying to put the sun in my travel bag." One has to go and look at the watercolor transparencies of the sun on the snow, the enamel sky of an incandescent blue, crossed by the transient line left by a plane, or shining from a glimmer of steel in the winter dawns. From Peru to Argentina, at an altitude of 3,000 meters, extend deserts of sharp rock and bare stone, the roof of the world, the high plateaus of the Andes, the altiplano. So flat that one discerns against the horizon the roundness of the earth, so high that one goes above the clouds on endless black or indigo blue roads, it gives one the bizarre impression of being an aviator without a plane and, as soon as evening comes, one can wander among the stars like Antoine de Saint-Exupéry's hero Fabien, lost in *Night Flight*. Once every hundred years, after spending a long time in the metallic earth, a prickly plant grows up, reaching over 10 meters, like a baroque church candle. From nowhere appear shadows as if carved out of the mountain, phantoms woven out of the chiffon of the mist—this one with its head bent forward under a woollen bonnet or a felt hat, running with small hurried footsteps, carrying his load in a blanket tied up on his shoulders; that one glued to the ground, squatting under his poncho, waiting for the unlikely passage of a

Page 48:
Andean landscape.

Page 49:
Atacama Desert,
northeastern Chile.

Pages 50 and 51:
Bolivian landscape,
province of Ingavi.

Opposite:
Upsala glacier, Bolivia,
province of Bautista
Saavedra.

Below:
On the railroad linking
Bolivia and Chile between
the cities of Uyuni and
Calama.

"Describing the cordillera would be like trying to put the sun into my travel bag."
Ricardo Güiraldes

Overleaf:
Bolivia, Lake Titicaca.
Tinted photograph,
Roland Paiva, 2001.

Above:
Straw market in Azogues,
Ecuador.

Below:
Petito Moreno glacier,
Patagonia.

Opposite:
Lake with Petito Moreno
glacier in the background,
Patagonia.

Overleaf:
Llano, Huarnuarco, Peru,
at the source of the Amazon
and the salt marshes
of Maras, 4600 meters.

bus or a lorry that finally appears suddenly in the dust from far away. The men are the color of the earth of the Andes in ponchos streaked in ochre, red, mauve, black, granite, basalt, quartz, porphry or sandstone. On the stony slopes frozen by the frost, their appearance follows or precedes that of gentle llamas, alpacas and vicuñas that appear to dance. Below, dry-stone walls topped with a thatch can finally be distinguished from the immense rock that they had appeared to be a part of. "Higher up," wrote Güiraldes, "a snow-covered peak, of a white so pure that it could be cut from a crystal made of time." Dazzling views of white in all its incendiary brilliance. Those of the highest summits, "the geological sphinxes," of which Güiraldes wrote that they were "prayers of stone . . . serenity made into matter, flight in lethargy. " That of the Bolivian and Chilean *salares*, whose salty crystals still bear the mark of the waters that covered them over 10,000 years ago; the brilliance of their phosphorescent whiteness is such that it is visible from the moon. That of the "huge mass of light" discovered by Humboldt and Bonpland when they saw "for the first time at last the South Sea," from the top of the Ecuadorian Cordillera. "A light that gave them an aura as if they were angels," wrote Jose Maria Arguedas. It was a biblical light from the chaos of the Creation, where the Earth began, in the breath of the wind: in Patagonia.

Patagonia

"The winds of Patagonia have tattooed my imagination with images both tragic and obscene," wrote Fernando Pessoa, who never needed to actually make the journey to feel the bewitching force of the winds there. The Alakakuf Indians had 30 different words to describe the different types of wind. Nine-hundred thousand sqare kilometers given over to contrary winds, including "the fastest on the planet," which "comes from the Pole like thousands and thousands of arrows of ice," noted Roger Caillois, adding that man walked there "tottering under the insistent pressure from the gusts of wind." The land of the devil, where man "must begin again the history of man." A land of nowhere. Desperately grey as soon as the snowy tides retreat. A land tormented by the winds that are filled with the free dreams of the ocean. Winds of salt, unceasingly distilling the poison of sterility, and fields of ice frozen by the great, angry winds. There are also petrified

"The winds of Patagonia
have tattooed my imagination
with images both tragic
and obscene."

FERNANDO PESSOA

forests—a prehistoric ossuary. It is a land of fire and hell, where, in the mud of archaic silt, the sea monsters withdrew to die. Horrifying storms sweep whistling through the high frozen passes. A land moving under the advance of glittering glaciers. A land of fire beneath a fixed star: the Southern Cross.

The Pampas

Below:
Ecuadorian harnesses
and lassos.

Opposite:
Gauchos in the
Argentinean pampas
taming wild horses, 1958.

"The gauchos only go out on horseback, even in their dreams, even to go from one room to another in the rancho or to go to heaven after their deaths."
Jules Supervielle

In this continent surrounded by oceans, dominated by mountains, invaded by virgin forest, encircled by the Equator, freedom runs through the plains where nothing arrests the gaze, whose gentleness alone relieves the solitude.

The gaucho would suddenly appear from out of the pampas, then plunge back into it as if into a sea that absorbed him and wiped away all trace of him. Indifferent to borders, the plain stretched out, uniform, around Buenos Aires and Montevideo, to the south of Brazil. "Unaware of the broken lines, the horizon waits patiently for him, knowing that, in a rush beneath the immense sky, he will go towards it," wrote the Uruguayan poet Jules Supervielle. The gaucho could be white, Indian or black, but above all of mixed race, speak Portuguese or Spanish, have an olive complexion and black hair, or blond hair and blue eyes . . . Did not one of them tell the writer Fernando Valdes that he had even known English gauchos? From the Indian came the poncho and the red scarf that he wore around his forehead to hold back the hair that he wore long, the bitter weed that healed even troubles of the heart, and the *boleadoras*—lassos made of straps weighted by three balls. From the Spaniard, he took the guitar that gave rhythm to his song of solitude and the horse, which was a part of him, the gaucho being "born" in the saddle. The untameable centaur was also a man-lyre, and therein resides all the ambiguity of his mystery. Created in the image of the pampas, the gaucho belonged to no ethnic culture, no people, no nation, nor even a group. He did not join or mix with others. Like the horses without masters that only the *boleadoras* could stop in their tracks, they went alone, and when they got together to lead a herd, or for a long night watch, squatting or seated on a cow skull around a fire of cow dung, they did so only due to chance meetings and for the basic pleasure of being together. Whether speaking Spanish or Portuguese, the differences between the languages were blurred by the gaucho dialect, which, as Borges stressed, was an intonation, an inflection, adding that "knowing how a person speaks is to know who he is; to discover an intonation, a voice, a particular syntax, it is to have discovered a destiny."

A poetic metamorphosis, it is through his disappearance as a real being, equipped with historical, economic and social dimensions, that the gaucho was born as a symbol of absolute freedom. The voices of numerous writers who knew how to capture and restore the spirit of the spontaneous ballads, born of the passage of the wind on the strings of guitars, "these couplets that come from inside like water gushing forth from its source," have enabled them to be written down, to be transmitted to the conquering city dwellers, imparting an eternal nostalgia for those who were eliminated

"My glory is to live
as free as the bird in the air
And no one has the right
to follow me when I fly off."

JOSÉ HERNANDEZ

They organized the same fate
for the man who had been
as invincible as a wild horse as for the ox.
"And where does the ox go
when it refuses to plow?" Martin Fierro asks
ironically.

Amazonia

It is difficult to apply the term "forest," as one would for the Black Forest of Germany or the forests of Canada, to the six million square kilometers which for the writer Paul Claudel had "almost the uniform consistency of an element," and gave Darius Milhaud, the composer, the feeling that "nothing had changed in this country since the first chapter of Genesis." Land? Waters? Since even before the land and the waters were separated. Virgin forest, destroyed more violently every day by the rapaciousness of order and progress.

Six million square kilometers of mystery was, until recently, impenetrable, remaining as the realm of the few Indians still pursued today, of the naturalist and the poet. Why? Because the naturalist examines everything through a microscope, and the poet imagines everything. "The size of the Amazon was such that it did not reveal itself before the 20th century," writes Milhaud, who, without any plane, explored part of it by boat and adds, "I have not seen the Amazon, so therefore I will not talk about it." *Terras dos sem fin*, "lands of the infinite," according to Jorge Amado. "Lands" in the plural because they are constantly renewed, constantly being reborn. Movable lands, the forest of a stage setting for an opera. It seems to stand on stilts, and no doubt this is the case, since, beneath the muddy red earth, its roots burrow down to the depths of what Claudel calls "the waters of the vast, primitive swamp."

The "Great Serpent-Mother of Men," as the Incas called the river, twists round the forest with countless tributaries and invincible meanders. River or serpent? It is a green hell of metamorphoses. Butterfly-orchids, insects with bodies of bark, leaves of praying mantis, cow-fishes, caiman-trunks, monkey-lianas, swarms of hummingbirds that look like the reflection of a rainbow, drifting islands and phantom hills swept away by the floods, rivers that are giant but so changeable that one of them bears the name "River of Doubt," enormous water lilies on which, it is said, jaguars drift down the river. "But these extraordinary appearances last no longer than the blink of an eye; immediately, the river, the forest and the grass close up on themselves, hiding their fauna, keeping their secret and their lives," Blaise Cendrars writes. In this forest, adds Ferreira de Castro, "the tree as such does not exist." It sometimes appears among the "tangle of plants, mad and voracious," high up in the humid atmosphere, hidden in the fog, with the shapes of Japanese calligraphic characters. All around, says Milhaud, is "a loud murmur that resembles silence." Deceptive Amazonia: its silence is false, its stillness false, swarming with hallucinogenic myths and

Opposite:
Orenoque River, Venezuela.

Below:
Cargo ship on the Amazon,
above the town of Teffe.

Overleaf, left:
The Manaus opera house,
which was constructed in
15 years and opened on
December 31, 1896.
Right:
The ruins of an abandoned
city in the jungle on the site
of the ancient city of Novo
Airon, on the Rio Negro,
Amazonas, Brazil, 2001.

Manaus and the grandiose Teatro Amazonas,
where Sarah Bernhardt acted in *L'Aiglon*.
The only theater outside Bayreuth
where *Parsifal* was staged.
In the lobby, tall paintings in imitation
of Aubusson tapestries that represented
"scenes of the forest."

poisonous treasures, shaken by lethal fevers and rotting dreams. Everything about it is part of a legend. Just like the haunted forests in the tales of ogres and fairies, it exudes legends like a bewitching potion.

To open the book of Amazonia is like opening the doors of the cabinet of Dr. Caligari. To the sound of the words of the smooth talker, to the rhythm of the lament of the hurling monkey, wailing out his foreboding at dawn and at dusk, rise the living attractions: Orellana and the Amazons, El Dorado and Aguirre, the rubber rush and the Mad Maria locomotive, firing rubber bullets for three hundred and fifty kilometers, with six thousand corpses of Indians who died building the railway inaugurated too late to be of any use, as the market had already turned its back on the black gold of the Amazon. The rush for cocoa, cotton, sugar, gold and diamonds, with the *garimpeiros* crawling around in the mud. The rush for wood, iron, copper, lead, coal, oil, bauxite and uranium. Staggering fortunes were made and lost, with no heed paid to the Indians, the slaves and the *seringuero,* "vanquished while the powerful looked on, as indifferent and impassive as the trees that watch us waste away from the fevers and from hunger, in the midst of the leeches and ants," wrote Jose Eustacio Riveiro in *La Voragine.* Splendid cities built and torn down, abandoning the carcasses of their glory to the forest. The city of Manaus and the grandiose Teatro Amazonas, where Sarah Bernhardt acted in *L'Aiglon.* The only theater outside Bayreuth where *Parsifal* was staged. In the lobby, tall paintings in imitation of Aubusson tapestries that represented scenes of the forest: feathered Indians, turquoise and pink parrots, toucans and caimans. An octagonal box, paneled with mahogany and beveled mirrors awaited Don Pedro II, the emperor dismissed too soon to make an appearance there. Manaus: a red dot on the maps in the middle of a green stain, crisscrossed with the black lines of the waters. Manaus, which took fifty years to be born, live and die, had sumptuous Carrara marbles, chandeliers from Venice, forged ironwork, robes and cognac from France, tea, shirts and tailored suits from London, automobiles and whisky from the United States, tiling and mosaic from Lisbon, all offloaded from steamers that chugged back and forth from Liverpool to the most isolated city in the world. Manaus, where 16 kilometers of avenues, routes leading nowhere and cutting off abruptly at the jungle, were equipped with electric tramways at a time when New York was still using horses. Manaus, where in 1897 telephones linked to the major stock markets of the world rang out everywhere.

This ephemeral city was a theatre of illusions, in the forest-continent where everything was no more than shifting appearance, the river-sea sweeping along its succession of adventurers, hermits, missionaries, witches, peddlers, explorers, runaways, whores and thousands of slaves.

People cannot go to Amazonia, they can only disappear into it, lose themselves in it, go astray, fall asleep, become passionately caught up in it, be engulfed by it.

Opposite:
Macaw parrot in the
Brazilian Amazon.

Overleaf, left:
Territory of Yanomami
Indians, region of Homoxi,
Roraima, Brazil.
Right:
A family of Kayapos Indians
from Para, Brazil, 2001.

"We think we are
in the Earthly Paradise."

AMERIGO VESPUCCI

66The adventure in the heart of
the New World signifies firstly that it wasn't
ours, and that we bear the crime of its
destruction; and secondly that there will
never be another one there.99

CLAUDE LÉVI-STRAUSS

CHAPTER IV

THE HORN OF PLENTY

Never propose to a peasant that you encounter along the way, his back bent double beneath his load, that you buy his goods from him straight away. As a practical and hurried Westerner, you would doubtless think that you were relieving him of a burden and also saving yourself time. But this would only upset him. In any case, he would refuse. All that you would be doing would be taking away from him the pleasure that awaited him at the market—an age-old and continually renewed pleasure, as important, if not more so, than the meager profit that he stood to make. In the towns, the markets take place on the parade grounds—the political, economic, religious and social centers of Latin America. Elsewhere, they seem to appear out of nowhere, at an altitude of three thousand meters, in the shadow of a volcano, on the shores of those emerald and azure lakes that materialize from time to time at the bend of an Andean trail. Everywhere, the local markets reveal splendors that bring to mind what Bernal Diaz del Castillo, the chronicler of Hernán Cortés, discovered for the first time, before the destruction of Mexico.

His description, full of wonder, spoke of a place buzzing like a beehive, where, forming a perfect order, each alleyway had its own specialty, offering up to the eye brilliant colors of woven feathers or cotton fabrics, nuances of the ochre, red and black clay of painted or varnished pottery, jaguar and buck skins, leather of roe deer and otter tinged white and red, knives of obsidian, skeins of thread, dyes of indigo or of the scarlet cochineal and, of course, gold and silver plate and stalls of turquoises, jade and precious stones. He also saw there strange fruits and vegetables unknown to Europeans and for which words had not yet been invented: corn, dried beans, potatoes from Peru, sweet potatoes, pumpkins, gourds, squashes, zucchini, cassava, tomatoes, avocados, pineapples, guava, papaya and all sorts of peppers. He saw aloe flowers, dahlias and sunflowers, and, of course, hundreds of medicinal herbs, tobacco and the cocoa beans with which all goods could be paid for. He even saw turkeys, which, like the Indians, got their name from the confusion between the new continent and Marco Polo's East Indies.

Revered throughout America, corn was a sacred food that was represented everywhere. According to the *Popol Vuh*, the sacred book of the Mayas, the first man, made of clay, was destroyed by a deluge; the second, made of wood, was destroyed by torrential rain; only the third, made of corn, survived. The Aztecs made ritual sacrifices of young virgins to their divine gods. According to the genesis of the Inca, corn and potatoes come from, respectively, the metamorphosis of the teeth and testicles of a demigod, born of the sun and a human female, so beautiful that his jealous father assassinated him.

Although Pablo Neruda saw in the potato "an almond of the earth, a buried rose, a flour of the night," the Europeans did not share the same poetic enthusiasm and, believing that it could cause leprosy in humans, at first reserved this foodstuff for pigs and for prisoners. It was in a camp in Westphalia that the prisoner Antoine Parmentier had a revelation about the tuber: he realized that the potato could save the population from famine and would have, as wrote Louis-Sébastien Mercier in his book *Tableau de Paris*, "the greatest influence on man, his freedom, and his well-being."

The tomato did not encounter as many difficulties, despite being of the same botanical family as the tobacco and potato plants. This was undoubtedly because it arrived via Naples, at the time owned by Spain, and its appearance of a golden apple—*pomodoro,* as it was named—seduced the Italians, ever willing to be seduced! The first ones were no bigger than cherries—the same type as those that have recently become popular again. Always suspicious, the Parisians waited before trying them in a sauce, making sure that the people of Marseilles were not poisoned by these apples of love, which were surely harmful since they were also called "apples of Paradise." Dunaud, Napoleon's chef, gave them a lasting place in his famous Marengo chicken. And then they finally took back their Aztec name of tomat(o). As for red fruits, we should never forget that the

Page 76:
Coffee plantation
of Candido Portinari, 1935.

Page 77:
Mexican market.

Opposite:
In Inca culture, corn
was thought to be the teeth
of a demigod born of the
sun and a woman.

Overleaf, left:
A Mayan market
in Chichicastenago,
Guatemala.
Right:
The inhabitants of Zunil
(one of the biggest Indian
towns in Guatemala)
go to the market
in Almalonga on the bank
of the Samala River.
This region is known
for its farms and orchards.

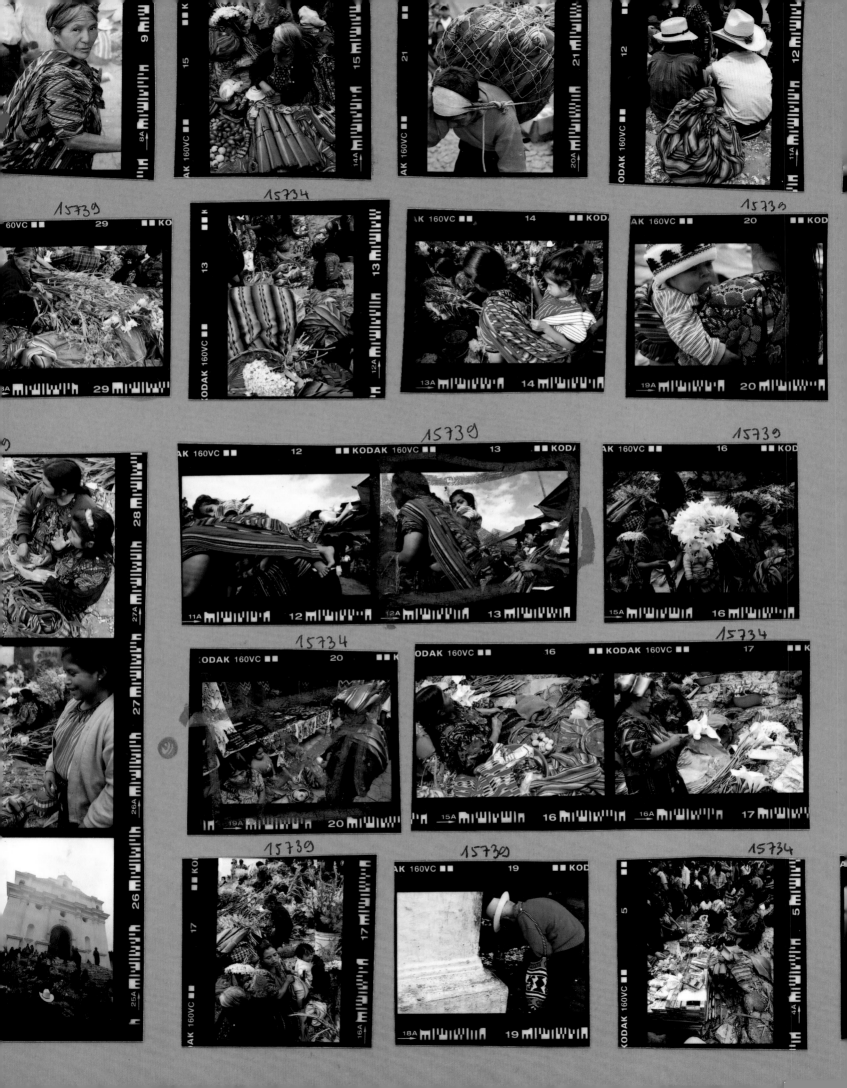

66To the Indian peasant farmer,
the market was his newspaper,
his theater, his means of
correspondence, a meeting place,
school, and university.99

GERMAN ARCINIEGAS

famous Plougastel strawberries, larger than average, were brought back from Chile in the 18th century by a Breton sailor, whom Providence had given the name Frézier (*fraise* is the French word for strawberry).

Chocolate

Biting into a piece of chocolate, smoking a cigar . . . insignificant, everyday gestures, with no mystery to them. And yet tobacco and cocoa contained much adventure—fortunes made and lost, dazzling towns that suddenly disappeared, the shivering of malaria or yellow fever, accounts of intrigues and crimes, of coups and revolutions. Memoires of slaves and tales of pirates, men's words and women's tears. The epic is all there, within that earth so red, at the bend of a raging river, beneath a vast sky, in the opalescent light of a tropical forest, in the unbearable sweatiness of a harbor. As soon as one enters South America, imperceptibly, the dismal indifference of manufactured products disappears in the face of the force of nature, the immensity of the plantations, the vitality of the country's legends and anecdotes, and the reality of everything. Like that painted by Giovani Basttista Tiepolo on the ceiling of the monumental stairway of the Würzburg Residenz, the allegory of America is often represented by a resplendent feathered Indian, smoking a long pipe, accompanied by a black servant carrying a cup full of steaming chocolate on a tray. A spell cast by mysterious America—like tobacco—chocolate first became known in the form of a drink. At first exotic, the new beverage quickly became erotic—an aphrodisiac love potion that was used to warm up the mood in the very libertine 18th century. As early as the 16th century, José de Acosta wrote in his *Natural and Moral History of the Indies* that chocolate "made the Spanish swoon." Like all things unknown, it was both attractive and repulsive at the same time; its appearance, and the passion it aroused—quickly compared to a contagious epidemic—as much as the ceremonial use that the Indians made of it, surrounded chocolate with an aura both disturbing and fascinating. Was it dangerous or beneficial? Divine or diabolical?

A symbol of prosperity and offering for the Mayas and Aztecs, who associated certain of their gods with cocoa, the privilege of drinking chocolate, served "in goblets of fine gold," was reserved for kings and caciques "to make them successful with women," noted Bernal Diaz del Castillo. Cocoa beans served as money, and another chronicler, Gonzalo Fernandez de Oviedo, specified that

Overleaf:
The festival of San Pedro, the patron saint of fishermen, near Lake Titicaca, Peru, 1991.

Below:
Les fruits du Nouveau Monde, *Jean-Baptiste Debret.*

Opposite:
Young estanciero on a plantation. The grim atmosphere of which Jorge Amado conjures up in his book Cacao.

84

"a visit to a prostitute cost between eight and ten beans." Oviedo dwelled also on the "ugly sight to behold" of watching people drinking cocoa: "It looks as if they are drinking garbage; its foam leaves brown marks around the mouth," and when it is red because it has been colored with annatto, "it looks awful because it looks like blood." For the Italian Girolamo Benzoni, it was a "drink for pigs"! This did not stop anyone from wallowing in the delights of cocoa: certain Indian lords in Nicaragua smeared their faces with it, removing some from time to time with their fingers, which they then licked. The beautiful Creoles, as the Whites born in America were called, tanned their complexions with a mixture of cocoa butter, clay and lime. Soon, a polemic arose concerning the vices and virtues of chocolate, with the debate taking on as much a medical as a religious tone.

At once "cold, dry, and melancholy," the "cocoa soil" also contains a fat that is "hot and humid, soft, soothing, and amorous," which "corresponds to the nature of the air," while the taste of cocoa is "bitter, of a subtle and penetrating nature" and has the hallmark of fire. Close to an alchemic analysis, the description by the doctor Juan Cardenas, author of *Problems and Marvellous Secrets of the Indies*, written at the end of the 16th century, would become the authority on the subject for the next two hundred years. It continued with a long description of the effects of chocolate, as contradictory as its properties, encompassing as many illnesses and diseases as it could cure. Did it take away the color of the person who abused it, leading to a state of debility? Or, on the contrary, did it fade on the skin as Madame de Sévigné assured her daughter, writing "The Marquess of Coëtlogon had so much chocolate when she was expecting that she gave birth to a little boy who was as black as the devil, who died." It was the Swedish naturalist Carl Linneaus who ascribed divine virtue to chocolate in calling it *Theobroma*—food of the gods. Honoré de Balzac, in his *Treatise on Modern Stimulants* published in 1835, was no less questioning: "Who knows whether or not the abuse of chocolate is implicated in the decline of the Spanish nation, which, at the time of the discovery of chocolate, was on the point of beginning another Roman Empire?"

Opposite:
Cacao trees in the hacienda
"Levante" in Chone,
province of Manabí,
Ecuador, 1912.

" Who knows whether or not the abuse
of chocolate is implicated in the decline
of the Spanish nation, which,
at the time of the discovery of chocolate,
was on the point of beginning
another Roman Empire? "

HONORÉ DE BALZAC

Tobacco

Opposite:
A colonial palace whose
garden was transformed
into a banana
plantation, Cuba.

Top:
Although the cigar is the
privilege of masculine
chic, the finest palates often
belong to women.
Bottom:
The salt marshes of
La Guajira, Colombia.
Salt is one of the numerous
riches from the South
American horn of plenty.

According to the very caustic Francisco de Quevedo, brilliant author of the Spanish gold century, "the devils of chocolate and tobacco" were the Indians' vengeance for the invasion by Spain, as it caused them more damage than Hernán Cortés or Francisco Pizarro. It was "the only new exquisite pleasure," wrote the sensual Pierre Louÿs.

From the thick and greedy lips of the big capitalists sent up in the caricatures of Otto Dix, to the sensual and generous ones of Che Guevara lighting his *puro*, the cigar acquired for itself a virtue, becoming, over the course of the century, the attribute of a dignity recovered through great struggle by the *barbudos*.

Since pre-Columbian Antiquity, tobacco has been, on American soil, a sacred herb, an attribute of the gods, the evanescent nourishment of the great spirits of the pantheon of many tribes. At Palenque, in Chiapas, dressed in a jaguar skin and wearing a Quetzal head, the smoking priest watches over the Temple of the Foliated Cross. For the Mayas of today, the gods of the Four Winds and the Four Directions remain great celestial smokers; mythological poetry describes lightning as being the spark from rocks struck by the rumble of thunder so that the fire destined to light the sacred cigars would burst forth; the shooting stars are only incandescent ashes; and clouds are smoke that bursts into rain. According to the Cuban writer Fernando Ortiz, smoking a cigar is still something magical and religious: "The slow fire that consumes a cigar is a rite of atonement. The smoke that rises to the skies seems to invoke the spirits. Its aroma, more seductive than incense, is a purifying form of it, the dirty but light ashes the mournful evocation of a belated penitence."

Does fate really exist? It was in Cuba that Columbus saw for the first time Indians carrying in their mouths rolls of dried and smoking herbs that they called *cohiba*. However, it was in the form that it was smoked by the Indians of North America—in a pipe—that it spread to the rest of the world. The sailor who discovered tobacco, Rodrigo de Xeres, on his return to Spain gave a demonstration: on seeing smoke coming out of all his orifices without his burning, the Inquisition believed it was seeing the work of the Devil and sent him to prison. When he came out again several years later, the whole of Seville smoked, and in those intoxicating wreaths of smoke the image of Carmen could already be discerned. As for Sir Walter Raleigh, who would never find El Dorado but who succeeded in converting the Court of England to the delights of tobacco, his

CHAPTER V

PASSION'S BAROQUE

Situated on the equator, Quito is a city of sharply contrasting light and shade. At noon, when the sun is at its zenith, the whitewashed domes of the Church of La Compañía appear suddenly like a snow mirage, burning white. Blinded, the earthly gaze becomes receptive to the celestial vision. Inside, everything is black, invisible, enigmatic. Then the eye perceives the shaft of light where color shoot's out brightly—the color of blood and tormented flesh. One by one, the stained-glass windows are set ablaze, pierced by the light of the sun. From all sides, the naked eye is seized, harpooned, hooked and terrified. On the glass poured into the heart of the lead, scenes from the theater of cruelty are brutally lit up, piercing the immense black naves with the obsessive obscenity of torture. Violent and sensual, the stately dance of martyrs exalts the ecstasy of torture to the point of hallucination. The divine nave becomes a nave of the crazy. Nothing is left to chance in the grandiose setting of the Spanish-American baroque.

Page 98:
Christ on the cross, Havana.

Page 99:
Colonial palace on Plaza
Mayor in Quito, Ecuador.

Overleaf:
Church of the Recolecci,
Antigua, Guatemala.

Top:
Sculpted christs,
polychromatic wood,
Ecuador.

Bottom:
Baroque columns, Quito,
Ecuador.

"There are a thousand churches per degree of latitude—70,000 between the tropics of Cancer and Capricorn," notes François Cali in his introduction to his very beautiful book on the art of the conquistadors, an art which he was among the first in Europe to explain was "also that of the conquered peoples," the transmutation of one faith into another and the alchemy between two arts, themselves nourished by different sources. On land that the conqueror appropriated by marking it with a cross carved on a tree trunk with the tip of a sword, the building of churches, which caused the power of the white man and the glory of his God to take root, was an urgent political and spiritual act. Royal decrees required that the first building constructed at a conquered place be a church; the design and the architect were soon imposed by the Council of the Indies in Seville. Peter of Ghent, the Flemish Franciscan, who claimed to have built "more than a hundred houses dedicated to the Lord, churches and chapels" in Mexico, maintained that "the Indians were only discovered in order for them to be saved." In 1539, his bilingual catechism, in Nahuatl and Castilian, was the first book printed in America.

During the first wave of the conquest, the Spanish were content with destroying idols and Christianizing temples. Small churches like those in Spanish villages were built of wood or with adobe, a brick made out of clay dried in the sun, however, the temples were then quickly destroyed. On their foundations, built with their stones, rose churches as large as the cathedrals of the Old World and overflowing with the wealth of the New World. The liberties taken by baroque art in Europe developed to their extremes in the vastness of America.

"Baroque" is the term used in jewelry to describe an irregular pearl. Beginning in the 17th century, the adjective was applied to objects with disproportionate shapes or of mixed materials and to paintings that did not conform to the classical canons of proportion. However, the term "baroque" was not applied

to architecture until the 19th century, when it was used by German art historians. In form as well as content, visually as much as religiously, baroque was the very language of the syncretism of interbreeding, going beyond the categories of art or of style to become a universe.

In America, Spanish aridity, constraint, asceticism, severity, rigidity and fanaticism were outflanked by the luxuriance, exuberance, gleam, abundance and frenzy of the indigenous landscape and spirit. What Elie Faure called "the tragic naturalism and the pitiless realism of Spain" collided with Indian animism, savagery and fieriness. The breeding ground for this graft was a common love of the morbid, the material was gold, and blood the living source.

The suffering endured, prescribed and glorified by missionaries around the world communicated directly with that of the Indians, beyond awareness or will. The drama of the Passion was internalized by these men whose terrestrial existence was nothing but the expression of the cosmic tragedy. The defeat of their gods and the massacre of their people made the survivors receptive to Christian redemption more than the monks' spreading of the good word. The teaching of the Scriptures was reserved for the Aztec or Inca aristocracy. For millions of Indians, liturgical imagery and spectacle replaced the Bible. The very carnal practice of Spanish Catholicism, the proliferation of its Christs, saints and Virgins; the propensity for mortification; the taste for relics and amulets dear to the missionaries (and close to fetishism); the mystical raptures of visionaries and the blessed; the proliferation of processions, services and masses—was naturally grafted onto Indian heritage, with its trances, sacrifices and blind submission to fate. Iberian Catholicism and Indian paganism trained each other, responded to one another, surpassed one another and raged with exultant suffering. Many priests and historians interested in the missions found similarities between pre-Columbian myths and Catholic mysteries as a result of tireless research. Despite its desire for transcendence, Spanish Catholic iconolatry remained close to pagan idolatry.

While architecture remained under European supervision, the ornamentation and the representations of the liturgical stage were the work of Indian artists and artisans trained by the Dominicans, Franciscans, Augustinians or Jesuits. The young Indian elite learned Latin, discovered Ovid and other classical authors. Through the Spanish monotheistic culture, this elite came into contact with other pagan gods—those of the Greeks and Romans, with the Dionysia and the Bucolics, with the serene art and the Classical canons of Phidias and Praxiteles, with the luminous and benevolent landscapes of the Mediterranean. From the Italian Renaissance, the Indian artist learned the shapes of the compromise that, in his hands, became a symbiosis. Between Ceres and Pashamama, what was the role of Mary? Between Inti Inca, Quetzalcoatl and Christ, the sun of justice, where did the divine light come from? It came from the unifying gold. It covered the questions that were too awkward for the Catholic hierarchy with a dazzling veil.

The gold plate that covered Inca temples, the precious stones that adorned Aztec statues and the funerary offerings and geometric mazes of pre-Columbian decoration resurfaced under the models imported from Renaissance Europe, blending into the Manuelino twists, Churrigueresque contortions and Moorish arabesques. Using the skill of Indian goldsmiths, the Creoles rivaled the vanquished gods and the Old World masters and overloaded church interiors with gold, silver and gemstones. Gold shimmers everywhere, often inlaid with mirrors that reflect the play of light and shade to infinity. Some of the silver or gold lamps, where candles imported from Spain burned all day, like the one in Copacabana, near Lake Titicaca, weighed up to 750 pounds. Under their gold vaults, the high altar and the chapels became the caves, *huacas* or mountains sacred to the

Top:
Commemorative plaque
depicting the Virgin.
Bottom:
Ornate coffered ceiling,
San Francisco convent,
Ecuador.

A Stiterunt

reges terre

principes conuenerunt

aduersus dominu

xpm eius. ps.

Andean peoples. Between the flowers, vines and palms that climb everywhere, clinging to every space, are hidden details only Indians can decipher. In the middle, in the heavy frames of gilt wood, rise the altarpieces surrounded by angels dressed in silk and lace who accompany the spirits of the trees and birds in their flight. And everywhere—splattered with blood, staggering, twisted, crawling, flagellated, crucified—Christ suffers. His chest opened to expose a beating heart, He is in the throes of a terrifying and perverse death, His eyes rolled upwards. In Cuzco, His wounds are rubies, the nails of His cross diamonds, and His crown of thorns emeralds. In the churches of the New World, to the sound of the bells and in the fumes of the incense, Spanish-Indian sacred art celebrates, in a mystical alchemy, the golden and bloodied wedding that produced the hybrid America. Who transcended whom, really?

The Half-caste Virgin

After 71 days of sailing, when they saw land flickering on the open seas, it was the "Salve Regina" that Christopher Columbus and his sailors sang in order to dispel their fear. When, after having braved a hurricane, Columbus finally arrived in Spain, he thanked she who is still called Our Lady of Silence at the sanctuary of Guadalupe—the place known as the "river of the wolf" in Arab-Andalusian patois. And during his second voyage, it was the image of the Virgin of Guadalupe that flew on the standard of Columbus, the Marane Jew, to protect and guide him. It would give its name to one of the West Indian islands, Guadeloupe. More than to the Father and the Son, the New World belonged to the Mother, she who, in this land of extravagance, gold, blood and pestilence, redeemed the vices of men, transfigured the humbling of women and glorified the suffering of slaves. She would become its official patron in 1760.

Our Lady of the Graces, Our Lady of Good Help, Our Lady of the Indulgences, Our Lady of Redonda, Our Lady of Loreto, Our Lady of Bala, Our Lady of Piedad, Our Lady the Conqueror and Our Lady of the Angels. The Virgin of Mercy, the Virgin of the Rosary, the Virgin of the Sorrows and the Virgin of the Remedies. *Tota Pulchra*—Totally Beautiful—the Virgin with a lily, a chair, a pillar, a rose bush, a mirror, a walled garden, a fountain, a star, the sun, the moon or a palm tree. The Virgin of Copper, the Virgin of Mining and the Virgin of the Silver Mountain. The miraculous Virgins of Copacabana, Oaxaca, Tepepan, Tolantonco, Zinacantán, Cancuc, Guápulo, Popayán, Belém, Catamarca, Caacupé and Alta Gracia. Madre de Dios. From Cuba to Chile, all over Latin America, the names of she who appears to save us from sin and from death resonate with the sound of celestial organs. From the 16th to 18th centuries, apparitions abounded, rivaling each other in terms of miracles and benefits. Whereas her Son remained irremediably white, the forever virgin mother knew how to

Overleaf, left:
Book of 15th-century
religious songs. Monastery
of San Francisco, Quito.
Right:
Church of San Francisco.
The Virgin of Quito is always
depicted wearing wings.

Opposite:
Virgin with rosary.
Monastery of Santa Catalina,
Cuzco, Peru.

Below:
The baby Jesus,
painted wood. Baroque
religious portraits depict
their subjects richly dressed.

Overleaf:
Church of Atoltonico,
Guanajuato, Mexico.

The Palace
of the Virgins
of the Sun
in front of
the Convent
of Saint
Catherine,
Cuzco.

get close to the vanquished, and became Indian, Black, mixed race or Morena. Only 12 years after the conquest of Mexico, the patron saint of the people of Latin America appeared on the Hill of Tepeyac, near Mexico City. In 1531, the Indian Juan Diego, a poor peasant, was guarding his flock there, close to the temple of the Aztec mother goddess Tonantzin, Our Mother, Mother of the World, also a virgin named Coatlicue, creator of the sun and moon. The site had always been sacred. Indians made pilgrimages to make offerings and sacrifices. It was there that, attracted by magnificent bird song, Diego discovered a Virgin with long black hair and coppery skin who ordered him to convince the Franciscan bishop of Mexico City to build her a church on the spot of the pagan temple. When he asked her name, she answered "Cuatlapcupeu"—she who comes from music and light like the fire eagle. Bishop Zumarraga twice refused to believe the Indian and asked him for proof. The third time, Diego unrolled his *tilma*, or cape, which was full of Castile roses that had just blossomed and were gathered on top of the hill, "where nothing grows but thorns" in the middle of December. Under the roses, on the rough fabric made out of cactus fiber, was the divine image on a crescent moon.

Unlike Our Lady of Guadalupe in Spain, who resembles the Virgin of the Apocalypse, the Mexican Madonna carries no child. Nothing—especially not her Son—would come between the Mother and her indigenous people. While Cortés immediately ordered a quest to build a church, Our Lady of Guadalupe only waited until the 17th century for her worship to be established, converting nine million Indians in six years, who, according to Franciscan chronicles, were "baptized with the left hand when the right hand was tired." She appeared at the right moment to mark the spiritual advent of autonomous Mexican indigenous Christianity. From an Indian Madonna, she became mixed race, attracting by her image a society fragmented by different combinations of racial mixing and its implacable social repercussions. Rising above the powerful—emperors or popes, archbishops or viceroys—she gathered under her vast starry mantle a people divided by the colorful patterns of interbreeding. This occured without conflict, and the Madonna served above all the interests of the *criollos*, Spanish Creoles born on Mexican soil and looked down on by those from Spain, who ruled the roost from the 16th century to the beginning of the 19th century. The Creoles insisted on the Indianness of Our Lady of Guadalupe; it was, however, the Indianness of the noble pre-Columbian savage, which the conquest caused to disappear, that was brought to the fore in the fiction of a voluntary conversion to Christianity on the part of the pagans saved by the direct intervention of the Virgin. The reality is completely different, and the Creole doctrinarians hijacked Indian devotion for a nationalist cause, which legitimized the conquest and the conquerors while justifying their thoughts of independence. By anchoring an identification, and a moral and spiritual justification in Mexican soil, Our Lady of Guadalupe allowed people to liberate themselves from the Spanish yoke and

Overleaf, left:
Virgin of the Sorrows
dressed in ceremonial garb
for the Holy Thursday
procession.
Right:
Church of the hacienda
"La Cienega" in Ecuador.

Opposite:
Virgin of Candelaire
(Virgin of the Gardens).
Guatemalan.

Top:
Virgin of Guadalupe,
anonymous, Mexico,
18th century.
Bottom:
Maria Ignacia of the Blood
of Christ, daughter of
the don Manuel de Oribe
of Sandoval, on the day
she took her vows
at the Franciscan convent
in Mexico, 1777.

became the symbol of the national unity of New Spain: Mexico. It would be wise to affirm that it was not the Indians who did the hijacking by endowing this Virgin with the role of the protective mother, in the shelter of which they continued to practice the faith of their ancestors. Our Lady of Guadalupe or Our Lady of Syncretism.

The Creoles prevailed, as did Mexico. In 1810, the rebel priests of the War of Independence, Hidalgo and Morelos, bore her image on the flags of republican liberty, while royalists preferred the Virgin of the Rosary. It was Pancho Villa and Emiliano Zapata, the heroes of the rebel army, who gave Our Lady of Guadalupe back her Indian and plebeian vocation. Bearing her image on the ribbons of their wide-brimmed hats, they made her the *pasionaria* of agrarian and social reform that they defended with their rifles. Finally, in the 1920s, in the face of the fierce attacks on the Church by the government and the passivity of the ecclesiastical hierarchy, the *Cristeros*, *guerrilleros* of Christ the King who came from the Indian peasant masses, fought shouting "Viva la Virgen de la Guadalupe." Throughout the 20th century, she would wash militant revolutionaries of the suspicion of communism. For millions of Chicanos, Mexican emigrants to the United States, she is the Madonna of the people, the patriotic mother who confers dignity and is the source of all hope and consolation. More recently, brushes of Californian artists have been turning her into a symbol of feminism. The continually changing Virgin, whom the people called the *Morenita* or "Star of the North", triumphed over both the Plumed Serpent and the Aztec eagle, over Cortés and Huitzilopochtli. Poetically analogous to the Virgin evoked by Octavio Paz, Our Lady of Guadalupe "battles and vanquishes the serpent and the eagle, and rises on the crescent moon."

Hence certain reversals of opinion and misunderstandings. "Pure-blooded" whites, Indians, those of mixed race, Blacks, *zambos*, slaves and the emancipated—Our Lady of Guadalupe, Our Lady of Syncretism, embraces them all and all claim to communicate in their common worship of her, even if each of them endows her with different virtues drawn from every religious and political source.

Opposite:
Procession in honor of the
Virgin of Guadalupe,
Chiapas, Mexico.

Processions

"Like a gush of purple sea in its phosphorescence . . . purple vests, purple shoes, hats filled the avenues with purple patches . . . an infinitely gloomy thing, like incense, the endless procession of wounds, the assembled wounds hurt the eyes, uniting the blazing aphrodisiac of the dense, dense human river . . . all of Peru was beating its breast." Such were Pablo Neruda's impressions in October 1947, on the holiday of Christ-of-Miracles in Lima, where, for three days, millions of the faithful don purple and carry their Savior from church to church along the narrow streets of the old colonial city. Twenty years earlier, Sergei Eisenstein shot images of the Holy Week and Corpus Christi processions in Mexico. In his journal, he noted the uninterrupted sea of faces bathed in sweat, the intoxication produced by the excessive monotony of the dance, with which, from dawn to dawn, from one foot to the other, the crowd swung at the same pace with a single, invariable rhythm. Strong and haunting images of flagellators in black hoods, white skulls, immense wooden crosses being brandished and Indians with haggard eyes devoted to suffering. Images burned by the sun into incandescent—almost transparent—white, all-absorbing black and diabolical shadows cutting with all the strength of evil through the innocent translucence of purified souls. Fervent Latin America.

Throughout the centuries, there have been many descriptions of the same scenes. The theater of a psychodrama, where the more cosmic mysteries of pre-Hispanic religions are played out at the same time as the Catholic mysteries, and where, every time, the positive and negative elements of the physical human element of syncretism are updated and put back together. The two traditions have fasting and physical sacrifice in common, as well as a taste for large-scale demonstrations of collective faith that bind the people to their religious and political leaders. As for the Aztecs and the Incas, they celebrated over 250 holidays annually. For the colonial authorities, the rigorous organization of multiple holidays, whether sacred or profane, were occasions to stage the grandeur and the strength of spiritual and temporal powers. It was a question of molding the imagination of the conquered peoples, of feeding it with new representations to replace forbidden beliefs and imposing new rhythms using a new calendar, the rhythms of the Western and Catholic temporality of Spanish public space. "The baroque procession is a sparkling mirror in which lavish Creole society admires itself; it is also the apotheosis of a

The appearance of the Black Christ during the Holy Week at Cuzco. The procession walks along a carpet of flowers made by the faithful.

militant esthetic in the service of colonial domination." Majesty, solemnity, rejoicing and elation "are its official watchwords." Attending processions was thus obligatory and sanctioned; the itinerary of the procession, its order and the sequence of all its stages were duly regulated, as was the participation of parishes, orders and brotherhoods according to the ethnic and social hierarchy. Paintings, tapestries, reports and chronicles allow us to imagine what these processions were like. They were at their most sumptuous in the 18th century—the apogee of the Spanish-American baroque—in which the interlacing of interbreeding exalted in the extreme, the licentious liaisons of the sacred and the profane.

Squares, streets, churches, convents, palaces, balconies and façades were decorated with heavy hangings emblazoned with brocade, statues, arches of greenery, palm trees, branches and flowers. In Mexico City, where the street of the goldsmiths was concealed by painted canvases representing the conquest of the city, the ground disappeared under the wet sand strewn with fragrant petals. In Potosí or Lima, certain sections of the route were paved with silver. There were platforms with red velvet canopies fringed with gold erected for the viceroy and the nobility everywhere. Altars were set up, covered in embossed silver plate, drowned in lace, floral garlands and gilt wood cherubs, collapsing under the enormous solid silver candelabras where pale candles melted. That was where the monstrance of the Holy Sacrament or the divine statues would make a stop. The procession advanced slowly, hindered by horses covered in velvet, bridled and shod with silver or even gold, by coaches in which, under the froth of organdy and cascades of pearls, wigged duchesses and marquises followed, accompanied by monkeys and black boys in gleaming silk livery. Gigantic silver crosses preceded the canopies. On the shoulders of guild representatives, sweating in their ceremonial garb, swayed the Christs, the Virgin, the saints made up with stucco, dressed in embroidered silk, dripping with jewels, wearing long hair that had been abandoned by novices, crowned with diadems encrusted with emeralds, their gold halos sparkling with diamonds. Escorted by archangels whose wings displayed the splendor of multicolored painting, the gods advanced through a crowd drunk with ecstasy, incense, heat, music and litanies. The baritones of the church bells blended their flights of low notes with choruses of chants and prayers, with the strident notes of horns, trumpets, flutes and kettledrums, and with the hammering of Indian drums. Mexican caciques or Andean Incas were dressed in traditional woven cloth, the vanquished worthies rubbing shoulders with the Spanish lord, the feathers of birds of paradise brushed against miters stiff with gold. Behind came the people of mixed race, from the lightest to the darkest, to whom the law forbade the aid of the parasol in order not to hide the stigmata of a sin that tainted a lineage to the sixth generation.

Overleaf:
Mayan purification rite,
Chiapas, Mexican.

❝There were
many to
shoulder
the idol:
multitudes
packed into
queues and
debouching
like sea water.❞

PABLO NERUDA

As for Holy Week, it gave rise to what are called "blood" processions. Nothing was spared to reinforce the conquests of souls and lead the new religion to the most intimate level, in the emotion of bodies. The Indians became actors and, led by the priests, especially Jesuits, experienced wholly the passion of Christ in shows of contrition, then of rejoicing, the sorrow at the death and the jubilation at the resurrection, moments of flagellations, lamentations, trances and dances. In his book on the art of the conquistadors, François Cali notes that "In Mexico, a willing penitent was really crucified, with real nails on a real cross, on Good Friday and died as a result." Fleshly bodies blended with those of the gods, made by these same Indians—Christs, Madonnas or saints whose eyes were filled with crystal tears, with real teeth, supple leather tongues, human hair, eyelashes and nails, articulated marionettes moved by springs hidden under their robes. A collective hysteria reached its climax during the crucifixion, when the wounds of the stucco Christ were covered with real blood that spurted from a skillfully hidden bladder. The dramas and joys of the Son, His mother and His companions lived in the deepest part of themselves. El Aleijadinho, the mulatto, bastard and leprous sculptor who attached his scissors to his stumps, captured these expressions of desperate faith. In Congonhas do Campo, the Brazilian province of Minas Gerais where, as in fairy tales, flowed rivers of gold, streams of diamonds and torrents of emeralds, 70 statues of the apostles, saints and servants have fossilized the baroque procession forever.

While religious festivals have sometimes lost ground in the capital cities to patriotic commemorations, they took refuge in the countryside where Corpus Christi and Holy Week are celebrated everywhere, where each village has its own Virgin or saint that is carried around at the slightest pretext. Elitist during colonization, festivals, processions and carnivals, largely reinvested with pre-Columbian cosmogony, have, with independence, passed into the arena of the people. They are, of course, no longer as sumptuous. Colored papers, golden cardboard, tin cans and fluorescent nylon have replaced the gold and the silk, but churches, statues, masks, representations and dances have remained the same—a godsend for anthropologists who, one after the other, dissect these celebrations in an attempt to identify their strata and to penetrate their labyrinths. Nowhere else in the world have these rites remained so relevant. In Peru, Mexico, Colombia, Ecuador and Guatemala, the sacred celebration has abolished the frontiers of time. It is, according to Octavio Paz in *The Labyrinth of Solitude*, the only luxury of peoples whom poverty and geographical isolation have deprived of other pastimes. Western tourists have included the best-known celebrations on their short, voyeuristic itineraries. Having escaped from the modern masses that, as Octavio Paz remarks, "are conglomerations of solitary persons," are they looking for "a living community in which the human being dissolves and finds his salvation in one movement"?

Opposite:
Carnival in Oruro, Bolivia.
Dawn ceremony (6 A.M.)
opposite the sanctuary of the
Virgin of Socavón. The mira-
cles of the Virgin of Socavón
are known beyond the
district's frontiers.
Both tourists and dancers
alike express their faith with
pomp and noise.

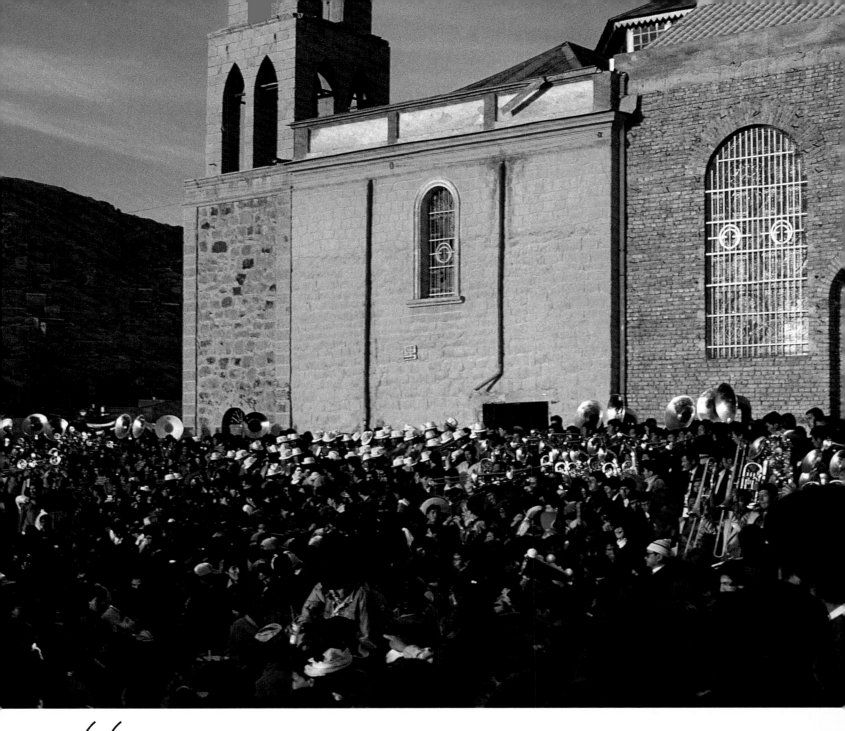

" **… a living community in which the human being dissolves and finds his salvation in one movement …** "

OCTAVIO PAZ

CHAPTER VI

MULTICULTURAL ORCHESTRATION

Celebrations go hand in hand with the image of Latin America. "*Armar una rumba, irse de mariachis, andar a la cumbia . . .*" There are so many dances, so many ways of saying "to have a good time." A radiant celebration of explosive and contagious joy has spread throughout the whole world, in a fusion of all its rhythms, already noticeable in the strong sounds of the names: rumba, conga, mambo, cha-cha-cha, guaracha, bolero, son, danzon, cumbia, marinera, calypso, samba, bossa nova, bamba, merengue, salsa. These names burn the ears, warm the blood in the coldest of veins and trigger movements of the body that are impossible to supress. It is at the heart of these words and rhythms that the driving elements and vital impulses bubble and swirl to give South America its exclusive type of energy— that which comes from a mixture of cultures. It is produced by those torn away from Mother Europe, the White conquest and colonization, in their double action of destruction and construction, having caused the uprooting of the American Indians and of a large number of Africans. They were thrown on top of each other by this terrible shaking down of earth and men, the gods, languages and cultures of three different bloods being squeezed together.

Despite the Europeans' desire for segregation, on the rubble of the great American Indian civilization and the ravages of slavery, the game of love and life quickly mixed colors and cultures together into a monochrome inifinity. Dance, doubtless because it is the language of sensuality; music, because it is the impalpable language of sensitivity; the poetry of sung words, because it is the language of the heart—all these become melting pots in which all the elements that fed the mixed culture were brought together and transmuted. From Cuba to Argentina, Rio de Janeiro to Lima, the persistence of the roots of this music overwhelm the energy of newer forms. Depositaries of the collective memory, the sounds, rhythms and words intertwine to infinity the figures of lost universes to create the multiple symphonies of the New World.

White, Black or Indian, forms of music and religions were thoroughly mixed in South America, going through many metamorphoses. Macumbas in Rio, Candombles in Bahia, Voodoo in Haiti and Santeria in Cuba, as well as innumerable lesser-known variants, were born of the syncretism of the different African rituals and their meeting with the pre-Columbian religions and Christianity. For the Africans torn away from their land, principally West Africa, the music that traditionally was a vehicle for gaining access to the divine being became the sole area of freedom. The small, trailing steps of the Colombian cumbia, which originated on the Carribean coast, tell at once of the constraint of leg irons and the liberation that comes from dance. The energy of the summoning drum, messenger between man and the gods, dominating the crossover rhythms, gradually lost its purely liturgical character to include secular music. Faced with successive structures of oppression put in place by the White order, musical expression was more than anything else an escape from domestication and control. Against proslavery depersonalization, the Africans grouped together according to their origins and created nations— societies of mutual aid and religious and cultural preservation, which were either tolerated, encouraged or supressed depending on the interest of their masters, and which survived beyond slavery. Music and dance gave emphasis to initiation and fertility rites as well as the rhythm of work in the plantations and mines. It exploded on carnival days and authorized celebrations, a release for passions, drives and popular feeling. Black dance and music were also used in the support and expression of numerous rebellions, some of which were successful and ultimately gave rise to the *palenque*, a free community founded by slaves who had taken refuge in inaccessible regions.

Particularly in evidence on the Carribean coasts, in Cuba and in Brazil, African heritage, as a result of the extreme mobility of the black population, has radiated with its multiple beats the American musical mix. The wind of revolt today is bringing forward urban adaptations of types of music that, evolving with the people, remain infinitely contemporary. If music is present everywhere in America and is constantly brought up to date, it is because it has always been the main popular art form and the most important of social ties. The intermingling of American

Overleaf, left:
Miss Oaxaca, Mexico.
Right:
Carnival, Rio de Janeiro.

Opposite:
Street in Havana, 1992.

124

Dance, music and poetry
are the crucibles of the alchemy of hybrids.
Sounds, rhythms and words are interlaced
with figures from lost worlds to create
the multiple symphonies of the New World.

Indian, African, Spanish and Portuguese folklores, the assimilation of different esthetics continually fed by contributions from new immigrants and internal migrations, has provoked a musical proliferation that is unique in the world. The history of American crossover music can be observed by looking at the inextricable entanglement of its musical strata, its surprising instrumental mixes, the steps of its dances, the words of its songs. A collective and often anonymous creation, it bursts forth from the spontaniety and improvisation of a community that has a destiny beyond its different roots. It is a music of the open air, of full voice, where the orchestra—or more often the band or fanfare—never plays alone, but is accompanied by exclamations and hand clapping in response to and returning its energy, and choirs that repeat a refrain spontaneously. It is a music made for dancing and partying, through which the poorest escape humiliations, frustrations and constraints, reawakening the vital life force of the earth. A direct reflection of society, the words comment on the events of everyday life, with an abrasive humor and a subversive lucidity, as well as with a poetry of feelings never afraid to reveal themselves. A source of distraction and happiness to those who have little else, the Latino dances burst forth still today, from the "rabble" of the villages or suburbs, and always start out being regarded with suspicion by the bourgoisie, who end up adopting them with enthusiasm, reprocessing and watering down that which it can no longer suppress. Alive because it is eminently popular, the Latino-American celebration brings together all generations and generously welcomes all forms of music. The advent of records and the omnipresent radio have never replaced the custom of dancing to the sound of orchestras, organized or improvised; nor is it rare to see, in the cafes and cantinas, people getting up to dance around a juke box or to accompany the "canned" music by playing on bottles or beer cans. Next to the new urban rhythms that, influenced by those of the Hispanic minorities living in the United States, have fused with rock or rap, like techno-cumbia, salsa-rock or Latino rap, which have swept across the continent, the traditional dances like the marinera of the northern Peruvian coast or the original Colombian cumbia still flourish. Innumerable, the various types of Latin American music return continually to their sources, changing instruments, shifting rhythms and melodies, integrating and adapting new foreign elements, creating new hybrids and enriching the global creation of music. It is like a musical geyser, constantly bubbling in a permanent state of fusion and mutation—the image of the continent itself. Although rooted in the furthest depths of their national particularities, certain of these types of music, although very different, have become universal: for example, the *saudades* of the Brazilian bossa nova, the *tristesses* of the Argentinian tango, the jubilations of the Cuban son, the *lamentos* of the Mexican bolero. No doubt because, more human than any other, they seize straightaway our innermost parts of ourselves.

Overleaf:
Rehearsal of the Trinidad
Folkloric Ballet, Cuba, 1998.

Opposite:
The world of tango
as depicted
by an anonymous muralist
in Buenos Aires.

The Bossa Nova

"Originating in Bahia, if today it is White in its poetry, it is Black, very much so, in its heart . . . " Thus the great poet Vinicius de Moraes characterized the samba in his *Samba da bênção Saravah*! Pierre Barouh took up this Samba of Blessing in *Un homme et une femme*, the film of French director Claude Lelouch, who was responsible for establishing the success of Brazilian music definitively in France.

The sung Samba is the softer, quieter sister of the carnival samba weighed down by the *surdos*, the big drums used to give rhythm to marches and processions. Descending from the *favelas* of Rio, where between the abolition of slavery at the end of the 19th century and the beginning of the 20th century, Blacks from the northeast looking for work gathered together, the wild samba was integrated into the urban atmosphere. It was enriched by the addition of instruments such as the saxophone and the flute, and proceeded from carnival to carnival to conquer the good districts, becoming one of the cultural symbols of Brazil. In this country that is as big as a continent, where, like the Amazon full of waste, the turbulent river of crossover music permanently stirs up new alluvial deposits, the music is of course mixed, and the styles of sambas multiply and meet, vying with each other. Having become a universal form of music in and outside Brazil, it took on a hint of cool jazz, becoming all the rage in Copacabana, Ipanema and Leblon, the hip beaches of Rio. Nor must one forget that from its cradle soared also the spirits of Heitor Villa-Lobos, Darius Milhaud, Maurice Ravel and Claude Debussy. In 1928, the writer Oswaldo de Andrade stated in his *Cannibalist Manifesto*: "Brazil is a carniverous flower that devours and digests all that is around it only to regurgitate it later in the form of a completely original creation."

At the end of the 1960s, three great musicians blended samba with the bossa nova—synonym of the new wave: João Gilberto, guitarist and sometime composer, sung or rather murmured words that Vinicius de Moraes, "poet and former diplomat," wrote for him to go with the music of a musician and avantgarde ecologist who would also become a poet, Antonio Carlos "Tom" Jobim. "He believes in the poetry of music and I believe in the music of poetry," said Moraes of his meeting with Jobim, who, in turn, wrote of Gilberto: "He is better than silence." According to the number that launched it in 1958, the bossa nova is the *Chega de Saudade*, daughter of saudade. The untranslatable saudade, of the Portuguese *fado*, an unpalpable bittersweet feeling, a clever dose "of a mouthful of sadness, another of hope," according to the words of Vinicius. In 1959, Jobim and Moraes composed the music of "Orfeu Negro," for which Marcel Camus would win the Palme d'Or at the Cannes Film Festival. The superb images and bewitching poetry of this first night revealed to a mar-

Below:
Scene from Marcel Camus'
film Orpheu Negro, *1959.*

Opposite:
Laura Vison, one of the most
famous transvestites of Rio de
Janeiro, 1991.

Overleaf:
Porto Seguro, Bahia, 1992.

“Originating in Bahia,
if today it is White in its poetry,
it is Black, very much so,
in its heart.”

VINICUS DE MORAES

Down to Rio? Those burlesque tangos that swept along Jack Lemmon and Tony Curtis in *Some Like It Hot?* Or that of Groucho Marx and his enormous partners, taken up again by Woody Allen at the end of *Everyone Says I Love You?* Or, finally, the grotesque, erotic and tragic tango of the last hour dreamt up by Bertolucci for Marlon Brando and Maria Schneider in *Last Tango in Paris?* None of these is the real tango.

These incarnations demonstrate, however, what Jorge-Luis Borges called its universal form—a form capable of taking on multiple aspects, of being, beyond a dance and a song, a completely separate dramatic art. "The tango can be discussed," wrote Borges in his *History of the Tango*, "but, like all that is true, it conceals a secret," adding that although a definition of it can be found in music dictionaries, "this definition is elementary and does not hint at any difficulties; but if a French or Spanish composer, confident of this definition, composes a 'tango,' he will discover, not without astonishment, that he has composed something that our ears—those of Argentinians—do not recognize, that our memories do not hide, and that our bodies refuse. One could say that without the evenings and nights of Buenos Aires one cannot do the tango and that in heaven, the platonic concept of the tango awaits the Argentinians . . ."

Born of Buenos Aires but adopted by Paris, which gave it the recognition that its city of origin refused, it was from France that the "scandalous" tango set out to conquer the world, to return triumphant to its home. Through the tango, Paris invented for itself Argentina, and Buenos Aires, fascinated, projected its impossible desire for Europe on France. "It is said that over there that those who know how to dance the tango marry millionaires," wrote Roberto Arlt in his novel *El Juguete rabioso*, published in 1926. "Over there" meant "the cities of the other side of the ocean," and of all of these, it was Paris, with which Buenos Aires had carried out an amorous love affair for more than a century, that became inscribed like a watermark on the history of the tango.

Top and page 140:
On the streets, San Telmo,
Buenos Aires.

Bottom:
Scene from the film Salsa
by Boaz Davidson, 1988.

The tango came from the suburbs where, at the end of the 19th century, were mixed together the former black and mulatto slaves, the gauchos—left over like cut pampas by industrial expansion—and the emigrants of European poverty, the majority Italians. Described as the "son of a guitar loved by two *bandonéons*" the tango is, for Argentine polite society, a "reptile of the brothel," as denounced by the writer Leopoldo Lugones. As legend would have it, however, it was one of the sons of a good family, the subtle and sensitive writer Ricardo Güiraldes, who danced the first tango in Paris, in the very fashionable salon of Madame de Reszké, in front of the Princess Murat and Reynaldo Hahn. If, as Albert Londres verified, the little French women "in the depths of despair" took off for Buenos Aires, the South American oligarchy was part of "le tout Paris" and even had there its magazine, *Elegancias*, run by the great Nicaraguan poet Ruben Dario. Proletarian in its own country, in Paris the coarse tango dazed an elite always eager for vivid sensations and which, on the eve of the Great War, gave itself over heedlessly to its exotic lasciviousness.

"Why is the tango not danced horizontally?" asked "Tiger" Clémenceau in his *Travel Notes in South America*. Tango lunches, tea tangos, afternoon tangos, supper tangos—1913 saw a dance explosion. Paris lived to the rhythm of the tango, dressed in the style of the tango. Corsets and clothing were softened and slit to allow a greater freedom of movement. The name "tango" was given to the Paris-Cabourg express train, race horses, a cocktail and perfumes. On discovering a stock of yellow silk damaged by humidity, which had turned it orange, a fabric merchant had the idea of putting it up for sale as "tango silk." People fought over it. What color other than that of fire could have been appropriate for this dance that set alight the Belle Epoque era with its sulfurous mood? The famous caricaturist of Parisian life, Sem, compared it to a sect, adding "half the town is rubbing up against the other . . . it is crazy about the tango." At the Académie Française, Jean Richepin engaged in a resoundingly learned praise, defense and illustration of the tango, viewed as one of the fine arts. With their hair brilliantined and waved, dressed up like the gauchos of operettas, Argentinian orchestras and dancers launched an assault on the capital, which soon boasted over 100 teachers. The war barely slowed down this passion for life, and although the Roaring Twenties saw the discovery of jazz, people continued nonetheless to submit to "the pallor of the tango that is sweeping away the South Americans—the color of cigars," as noted Louis Aragon in *Les Beaux Quartiers*. As reported by one of the greatest authors on the tango, Enrique Santos Discépolo, cited by the essayist Nardo Zalko in his book *A Century of the Tango: Paris-Buenos Aires*, "never have there been seen so many gauchos in Paris . . . improbable and inexplicable gauchos, in lamé with huge velvet flowers . . . in sailor suits embroidered with little boats or entirely encrusted with precious stones . . . !" In Florida, Carlos Gardel, the son of a laundress from Toulouse, sang in 1929 in front of Josephine Baker, Maurice Chevalier and Fujita, and carried off an undeniable triumph, while the troupe of the Moulin Rouge was applauded in Buenos Aires, where all the cafés and cabaret clubs took the names of French ones and replicated their decor, such as the Armenonville, the Palais des Glace and the Ba-Ta-Clan.

And the tango? It was finally launched in Argentina, which followed all the Parisian fashions, by musicians and librettists who were also marvelous poets. It even became the language of Buenos Aires, "a sad thought that is danced," as crystalized by Discépolo. If Argentina, with hair so black that it was blue, with its velvet look and sensual voice, was sweeeping through the Paris salons, the "sentimental

and charming French girl, a strange blend of Musette and Mimi," overconfident, went to Buenos Aires, becoming there a fleeting queen of tango, a favorite in the brothels, an object of desire, taking on an aura of the bewitching sparkle of the electric nights of the bright city. Mimi, Margot, Manon, Ninon, Fanfan, Vivian, Charlotte, Marion, Lulu and Madame Yvonne . . . the words of tangos are studded with the names of these beauties of the Parisian streets, prostitutes doused with champagne, who faded all too quickly.

Paris magnetized Buenos Aires. In an almost cubist collage, Paris between the wars, which was bohemian and sophisticated, as in the films of Georg Wilhelm Pabst or the ballets Russes, came into contact with other settings through the tango; namely with the reality of a proletarian Buenos Aires, which was proud of being so, with the magic of the matches struck by the Little Match Girl from the *Tales of Hans Christian Andersen*. Words like *champagne*, *corset*, *lamé*, *crêpe*, and *soirée*, that instantly evoke sensuality and refinement, became intertwined with the male, brutal, and rough tones of *lunfardo*, the slang of Buenos Aires to which Jorge Luis Borges paid tribute in his "The Sect of the Knife and of Courage." In a language traced as if by a tattoo knife but perfumed with Rose de France, are written works of a poetry that was never invented, because it had always been sensed. Here the heart is pierced by a poisoned arrow of betrayal. If one laughs or becomes intoxicated by it, it is only in order not to cry. Love is a fatal bewitchment, born of the night torn apart by the sharp flash of a blade. Passion flees with the dawn, not without having left its red mark "coagulated to black," unless it is "this crimson blood that stains souls". The settings, the symbols, the accessories, the characters, the situations, all the imagery of the tango could be ridiculous, except that it is the only melodrama that is not. Because above all else, it pokes fun at itself, with the awful baroque humor that marks not only Argentina, but the whole of Latin America. Desire, violence, defeat, desertion, the lament of the *bandonéon* exalts the bitterness and gives a rhythm to the derision. "In the end, who is guilty of this grotesque life?" asked Homero Manzi of the tango that he dedicated to Discépolo, for whom "life is a sepulchre of dreams, and we are but façades of what we dream of being." The tango is a nostalgia—not the regret of a better time, but the pain of being uprooted, the inaccessibility of being otherwise, the exile of oneself, the eternal striving to return without ever being able to. The tango speeds up life like a memory of a future that remains a dream. If the dance is a form of geometry softened by the body's describing over and over the equation of the relationship between man and woman, the tango is, in its texts, a metaphysical representation of human tragedy. Through the image of its figures, everything is played out in self-control, restive captivity, the flux and reflux of a mortal eroticism made of dazzling embraces immediately thrown apart, which represent so many misunderstandings and so much solitude. Like no other dance, like no other song, the tango speaks of the couple, of its hopes and fears, the harmonies of its fugues, too quickly put out of tune by the turns of destiny, "life is an absurd wound and everything is so fleet-

Previous pages:
In La Boca, a neighborhood
of immigrants from Europe,
especially Italy,
the tango is still associated
with a primitive
and anti-establishment tango
danced in the bordelos.

Opposite:
Reconstruction
of a thirties dance hall
in a dance school
in Buenos Aires.

142

" Why isn't the tango danced vertically? "

GEORGES CLEMENCEAU

ing." Although the tango is so fascinating, it has become a legend whose universality extends beyond its *porteñas* roots, because it reveals and exposes, through the naked truth that its plebian origins allow it, the age-old archetypes of man and woman, "the all-absorbing love of a tyrant, jealously guarding his dominion over women who have surrendered submissively, like obedient beasts. The complicated laughter of depravity," wrote Ricardo Güiraldes in his very beautiful poem "Tango . . . Dance of Love and Death. Yes, but as Enrique Gonzalez-Tuñon would write on the death of Carlos Gardel, "when a singer dies, sometimes a dream is born."

The Cuban "son"

On the one hand bitterness, anxiety, derision beyond despair; on the other, softness, good humor, tenderness beyond sadness. Cuba and Buenos Aires, the island and the city, the earth and the asphalt, son and tango, as different as instinct and the metaphysical.

A correspondent in Paris for the Cuban magazine *Carteles*, Alejo Carpentier, told how at the beginning of the 1930s, thanks to Don Barreto's orchestra, the rumba, the first offshoot of son, dethroned the tango in the cabaret clubs of the Rue Fontaine. "Having had its fill of the stories of pimps who had stolen the savings of their girls to go to Buenos Aires and of shopgirls who would give anything to dress in percale," Paris deserted the tango cabarets. The *bandonéons*, let down, were inconsolable "But this is not music!" cried the *tangueros*. This was perhaps not music because it was much more than music; fragments of an infinite rhythm, meteorites that had become detached from cosmic time-pieces. Light and impertinent, the son is a happy song that is danced to a percussion rhythm. Exploding all over the Carribean, its Cuban source was the black province that in Cuba was called the "Oriente" and whose capital, Santiago, mixed the musical torrents of the African *yoruba* and *abakwa* with the Andalusian Moorish and gypsy flamenco. During three hundred years of colonialization, close to one million African slaves were taken to Cuba to work on the sugar and tobacco plantations. They made music with everything that came to hand: donkey jaws, spades, ploughshares, crates, spoons, jugs, and frying pans. The great musicologist Émile Vuillermoz analyzed at length "this orchestration that is very close to life, that seems to be the universal consent of things to the rhythm of dance." Recently rediscovered thanks to the film *Buena Vista Social Club*, the son has always existed, but was crystallized in 1920 into what Alejo Carpentier called "its pure form." As for the rumba—or rather rumbas, as there were several forms—Carpentier noted that no one, not even its musicians, could really define it. "All the constituent rhythms of Cuban music are included in it," he added, adding that "more than a type of music, it is an atmosphere," which takes on a different form from village to village, with improvisation being of great importance.

Opposite:
Cuba, province of Havana. The Malecon is the long avenue that runs along the sea.

144

Imperturbably loyal to the traditional son, Eduardo Rosillo was the venerable producer and presenter of the program "Alegria de Sobremesa," an institution of Radio Progreso, which started up in Havana in 1929. It is thanks to him that the scattered members of the Buena Vista Social Club were able to be reunited; in the mazes of destiny, he had not lost track of them at a time when they were disappearing: judged insufficiently militant for the Maximo Leader, the "sones" had given way to more educational choirs. Every day, the public recording of the program attracted young and not-so-young fans. In an ancient studio, where the air conditioning often broke down or, on the contrary, delivered a Siberian cold, the program started off with a serious listening to old and new groups, old and new records, "for José to celebrate the birthday of his beloved." Very quickly, people began to dance between the seats to the sound of the Aragon or Van Van orchestras. It was like being at the Salon Rosado de la Tropical, an enormous open-air dance hall, where orchestras and DJs came on one after the other without a pause, and where, with all the different generations mixed together, one could dance day and night. Rosillo explained that, in words and music, the sones flowed spontaneously from everyday life, that they were not thought up or composed, but felt and then translated into a musical language. This was the secret of an inexhaustible creativity. The other secret of the son was that it remained a purely acoustic music that—a thing more and more rare—all the musicians recorded together. It was an artisanal, rural music, at the heart of all mixes, of colors and of ages, a music of companions, of friends—*compadres*—from whence came the nickname "Compay," a music about the joy of living, loving, and creating together.

Below:
Santiago, Cuba, 1996.

Opposite:
Compay Segundo and the
Buena Vista Social Club.

Overleaf:
Musicians, Havana.

From the son derived the rumba, the mambo, the cha-cha-cha and the salsa, which would spread throughout the world. In 1956, the film *Et Dieu créa la femme* came out. The bass player Israël Cachao Lopez had created the mambo in 1939, which the pianist Perez Prado popularized in 1950 and Brigitte Bardot and Silvana Mangano used to tug at heartstrings. Four years later, in Henri-Georges Clouzot's *La Vérité*, Bardot launched the cha-cha-cha, invented in Havana by the violinist Enrique Jorrín. At the intersection of Broadway and 52nd Street, the Palladium Ballroom was, from 1954, the Latino heart of New York, where there existed a rivalry between the orchestras of the "two Titos"—Puente and Rodriguez. Masculine counterpoint to the Carmen Miranda of the big screen, the amazing Dario Moreno (originally from Turkey) led the 1960s joyously in a South American frenzy everywhere and in all forms. After the "Cucaracha," "Guantanamera" became a hit

" Our song is like
a muscle beneath
the skin of the heart. "

NICOLAS GUILLEN

record; everywhere people were hopping to the bamba. At L'Escale, the group Los Machucambos shook their maracas and stirred up the crazy nights. At Saint-Germain des Prés, Bobby Lapointe made fun of it, humming his "Cha-cha-cha des thons avec un 'c' comme crocodile." The exile of numerous Cuban musicians to the United States following Castro's rallying to Communism, would give a boost to the Latino minorities. The son merged with, notably, the merengue of the Dominican Republic, the Puerto Rican plena and the rhythm n' blues of black Americans. This gave rise to the salsa—the sauce—as its name indicates, a socio-cultural fusion from which flowed a heterogeneous, unrivalled form of music, constantly reworked. It was always on the rhythmic base of the son, which, like Compay Segundo, had had a hard life!

The Bolero

"It is the story of a love affair" that gets under the skin, devours the depths of one's being, subjugates reason and sets free the senses so that they are given over totally to the happiness and unhappiness of loving. "The Taste of You," "Frenzy," "Slave," "At Your Feet," "Obsession," "Love Is the Bread of Life," and, like it, a vital need that is never satisfied. But although bread can be earned by the sweat of one's brow, tears of blood may be shed in pursuing the illusion of a love that one is never sure of winning. There's no knowing—it is an "obsessive dream of absolute and everlasting love," according to the definition of the film-maker Carmen Castillo, creator of a very beautiful film on the bolero's lessons of love. And it is certainly this that the dance is about—an education in the ways of love, which takes one through all the stages of passion: veneration of the beloved, sacrifice and torment, entreaties, despair and savored suffering, but also hope, atonement, redemption, a renewed miracle. "Without you, the night grows dark . . . I was born on the day I met you . . . Blessed love, I am searching for a refuge on your miraculous altar." If the bolero explores and exploits all the terms of Christian passion, it is because it is itself an oration of love that belongs more to the world of brothels than the Church. It is a confession as well, which, in defiance of immodesty, exposes all states and reveals all the figures of Love with a capital "L," including its filial, parental and patriotic variants. It is not by chance that the bolero, urban brother of the son originating from Havana, left from there in the 1920s to conquer post-revolutionary Mexico. Through the innumerable brothels that accompanied the wave of rural migration towards a capital in full expansion, it became, along with the social explosion of the Mexican revolution, the liberation of morals—the language of the new urban culture. Quickly moving on from the brothels that served as incubators of its first composers and performers, including the immense Agustin Lara, it gave rise to the creation of innumerable cabaret and dance halls, inspired theatrical plays,

Opposite:
Dancing the lambada. Created from a mix of Western music, this dance is inspired by the rythms and sound of the Carribean.

151

radio series, romantic photo stories and film scripts. Broadcast over the radio, the voice of Lara, who composed live at the microphone, was spread throughout the continent. On the blazing wings of the Mexican cinema, the bolero soon spread to Colombia and Peru, to Chile and Venezuela, becoming a cultural institution rooted throughout the whole of Latin America. It was a romantic song, "a way of being in love that has moved between people since the 1930s in every corner of the Latin American continent," said Carmen Castillo. From the shoe shiner to the doctor of philosophy, from the servant to the boss, the bolero is the common language of love, of a love in its unrefined state, set alight by the senses, stronger than oneself, stronger than everything, a kingdom of emotion in its pure state, where all social conventions are abolished. It is a fevered and torrential passion to which one abandons oneself entirely in the inescapable fatality of desire, in the dangerous pleasure of belonging to another. It is torrid and fleeting embraces, a wild sensuality sublimated by fairy tale images, beatings of the heart and the blood punctuated by the languorous music . . . *Besame, besame mucho* . . . Through trembling voices of satin or velvet, with a feather soaked in rose water and syrup, the bolero pursues an impossible love on a road inevitably strewn with betrayed loyalty, lost illusions, mortal possessiveness, agonizing jealousy, exhilirating hate, derisory sarcasm, implacable vengence, dignified forgiveness, painful healing and nostalgic oblivion. Carried away by the heart of a body without mercy, intertwined, held tight, glued together, the bolero couple whirl until their decline . . . until the next song, until the next miracle.

There is no right age for the bolero, which no other type of music has succeeded in displacing in Mexico, and which is taken up by young singers without casting any shadow on the success of the large and aging ladies covered in jewels, of fading tenors in pastel suits and bow ties, welcomed as heroes by the crowds that line up as whole families at the doors of provincial cinemas to hear again and again the same songs of Lara, Armando Manzaneros and Consuelo Velazquez. The bolero is the poetry of those who can neither read nor write, but who know the words by heart and thanks to them can put words to their lives. The expressions are so true that they have become a code from which intellectuals and writers have borrowed.

Opposite:
An open-air dance hall in
San Salvador, on a beach a
few miles from the capital.

Gabriel García Marquez described his *Love in the Time of Cholera* as a "200-page bolero."

CHAPTER VI

CAUDILLOS AND LIBERTADORES

Caudillos and *libertadores*—dictators and revolutionaries—haunt the history of Latin America as well as its literature, its myths as well as its reality. Following closely on the heels of the giants who led rebel Latin America and threw off the Spanish yoke, the regional *caudillos*, or leaders, appeared spontaneously. Natural leaders, whose charisma was linked to their war exploits, their authority was acknowledged instinctively—like that of a father. While Simón Bolívar, El Libertador, San Martín, the Just, and José Martí, the visionary poet, dreamed of a Latin American destiny and represented, in the words of German Arciniegas, "more than armies, ideals on the move," the *caudillos* were firmly fixed in an archaic rural world that was wary of republican ideas associated with intellectuals deemed too urban and too "European." Like Rosas in Argentina, Francia in Paraguay or Páez in Venezuela, the *caudillos*, carried along by the enthusiasm of the people, came to fill the power vacuum of a society emancipated from the institutions and norms that had always governed—free, but left to its own devices without any education that could have ever prepared it for this. Very quickly, these men, "just the men needed," whose discourse was always populist, betrayed, usurped and confiscated. The ownership of land and industries and a monopoly on the main products and services—taken over for their own benefit from former colonial privileges—made these "benefactors" not only the masters, but also the proprietors of a country run like a family business.

They opened up the way to a long line of despots, bloodthirsty generals or civilian autocrats who, from the Mexican Porfirio Díaz to the Cuban Batista, via so many other "illustrious Latin Americans," subjugated the continent—"consular" *caudillos* in the pay of and at the disposal of the United States.

Perpetually betrayed, bitterly disappointed, Latin-American people have never stopped rebelling against their tyrants. Sudden explosions, insurrectional movements instigated by an avant-garde that often included many intellectuals and artists, peasant revolts, military mutinies, workers' strikes, student riots, open or underground guerillas, all relentlessly kept any attempt to establish totalitarianism in check. This was the doing of anonymous and splendid sacrificial victims who were often victorious in putting an end to successive dictatorships, but who, because of the imbalance of power and economic alienation, could rarely vanquish them outright. The mechanism for underdevelopment that was imposed from start to finish was brilliantly dissected by the essayist Eduardo Galeano in "The Open Veins of Latin America." From Martí to Sandino, from Zapata to Guevara, from Romulo Gallegos to Salvador Allende, dreams of democracy have crashed into oligarchic rapaciousness and the intransigence of North America, as well as into corruption and widespread poverty, into terror, torture and disappearances. Latin America's apparent "instability" is only the result of the constant arm-wrestling between oppression and freedom.

The Dictator

Overleaf, left:
Caricature of General
Victorio Huerta, interim
president of the Republic of
Mexico, which appeared in
Le Monde illustré *in 1913.*
Right:
Bust of Jorge Eliécen Gaitan,
the populist candidate
in Colombia's presidential
election who died in
mysterious circumstances
in 1948.

Opposite:
Anatomy Lesson, *1969,*
by Carlos Alonso
(1900–1999).
The artist depicts torturers
in dictatorships.

After having lost a leg
in the battle of Veracruz,
fighting against
the french army in 1838,
the Mexican dictator
Antonio Lopez of Santa Anna
buried the dismembered leg
with great pomp during
an honorary mass
at the cathedral of Mexico.

In a single sentence, which, at first reading, may only appear funny, absurd or surreal, the humor of Gabriel García Marquez contains and projects all the tragic dimension of a phenomenon that, without being exclusive to the region, is however an essential component of Latin American political life: the *caudillo*. More profoundly, more completely than any political analysis, with a sensitivity and an intensity unknown in documentary accounts, the writers of the continent have, since the 19th century, covered, in the substance and intimacy of real life, all the circles of the hell where the devil is a dictator. From the reading of these numerous sociological novels, where fiction tries to moderate or make up for a reality whose abjectness will always get the better of it, emerges a profile of the *caudillo*.

As the Paraguayan author Augusto Roa Bastos advises in *I, the Supreme,* one must distinguish between the "The physical person and the incorporeal figure of the *caudillo*. One can get old and die. The other is constant and perpetual." Of little significance are the names of resident dictators who, without exception, were rife in all the countries of the continent. Like their busts and statues, which were knocked off their pedestals in turn, their names were lost in the dust of history. "And who was this man? . . . There will probably be no-one to answer. . . . He will be like one of the roman sculptures of a decadent era that may be seen in several museums. . . . A Gladiator. A Patrician. A Centurion. The bust or statue of a Dictator." And the *caudillo* in the

"—What time is it?
—Any time you want it to be,
general."

GABRIEL GARCIA MARQUEZ

158

Cuban writer Alejo Carpentier's *Reasons of State*, crying over the *Who's Who* that will never acknowledge him. Unless assassinated by their successor, the usurper of the usurper, and their corpses torn limb from limb to songs of elation, joyous firecrackers and the unbridled ransacking of their palaces, these immortal presidents would, in exile, join "the brotherhood of old, nostalgic dictators," depicted by García Marquez in *The Autumn of the Patriarch*.

Alive, the tyrant was invisible, though his image was in evidence everywhere. While he let himself be glimpsed by the people, it was only from a distance, and here and there—a rare appearance—in the back of a limousine, in the corner of a dark box in the dress circle from which he could see without being seen, from the top of a balcony "isolated from everyone, far away, surrounded by his close friends," like the Señor Presidente of the admirable and terrifying book by Miguel Angel Asturias.

An ancient general, president for life, he is as old as his power, he is the Patriarch: "As Supreme Governor, I am also your natural father." More than his features, that which is striking in him are the constant characteristics common to his species and, above all, a gaze that no one could resist. Magnetic and impenetrable, the *caudillo* is endowed by a popular belief that he inspires and maintains supernatural powers, almost divine, which are manifest via omnipotence.

The foremost of these powers is, of course, sexual. Both father and son of the people, of "this nation to which I gave birth and that brought me into the world," he is also its Don Juan; necessarily and systematically full of virility, macho and even more macho, he exercised his *droit du seigneur* on the country's entire female population. The indubitable proof of his inexhaustible potency is his multitude of illegitimate children. A Venezuelan tyrant even fathered some into his nineties. An outstanding lover, the *caudillo* really only respects one woman: his old mother, whom the people are requested to revere as a saint.

The supreme guide, great conductor, perpetual dictator, benefactor, savior, father of the country, restorer of independence, champion of world peace, protector of culture, of students, of the working classes, of abandoned women, he watches over his people with the love of a father, guiding the country to the vanguard of progress, and spreads happiness. "Here, we have a revolution on the move. I am the leader of the revolution," declared the supreme leader. "Here is someone who can do anything!" shouted the patriarch, a cry that reverberated like an explosion of power. "God and Trujillo" proclaimed posters praising the master of Santo Domingo. In order to govern, there is, "no need of an intermediary between the nation and the supreme leader. No competitors . . . as I want only to do good, I want nothing to stop me from doing so. He was the government unto himself and no one disrupted his will by words or deeds," wrote García Marquez. The *caudillo* never consults the people; he is aware of them.

Alone with the country and power, he assumes the heavy responsibility of defending order and progress, peace and public tranquility against the enemies within, as well as those without. A natural product of the masses, he suspends the

Opposite:
Workers' parade,
Mexico, 1926.

Below:
Christ as a guerrillero,
Chile, 1971.

159

state of emergency only exceptionally, during the rite that renews the plebiscite of the "most illustrious constitutional president of our time." "I proclaim myself candidate to the presidency of the republic with my pistols, without the involvement of parties or of a program," announced one of the general-presidents of Mexico. Omnipresent, "the *caudillo* decided on the spot and in person the tiniest details, governed in person at any time and everywhere." Written law? "What a load of rubbish! . . . A leader with guts does not let scraps of papers dictate how he should act. theory always gets messed up by practice," affirms Alejo Carpentier's dictator. "I put the excellent constitution of 1861 in this pocket and that of 1868, which was even better, in this one," exclaimed a dictator in the Bolivian congress. "Que viva el macho!" responded the frenzied crowd, requisitioned under surveillance to acclaim the manifestations of his complete power and total devotion. Whoever put forward the slightest dissident opinion was a traitor to the homeland. The patriarch is more than invincible, invulnerable not only to slander and attacks, but also "to time . . . to the plague and to cyclones." His secret? Supremacy. "I don't write history. I make it. I can remake it according to my will, adjusting, reinforcing and enriching its meaning and truth."

Armed forces, private militias, bodyguards, secret services, ministers, deputies, senators, judges—who had a finger pointed at them according to the *caudillo*'s whims—interests and even digestion participated in the staging of total power. All of them were compromised by the blood on their hands, which, as in the Mafia, constitutes the greatest proof of loyalty. The patriarch doesn't get a moment's rest, because as long as he has to be wary of their ambition, he keeps the most dangerous close to him in order to keep an eye of them. Constantly on the lookout, he keeps his entourage on the alert. "The rule of conduct of Señor Presidente is to never give anyone hope, to trample them all, to punish them all, simply because. The one who keeps his job is there because he does what he is told," said Augusto Roa Bastos. The militias of the dictator get rid of those they need to and disguise all traces. Thus would decree the patriarch, anticipating the very real policy of "disappearances": "I declare by supreme and irrevocable order that nothing happened here." Absolute domination, summed up by an image from the very popular Tarot deck, of which the supreme leader held the four aces that always won: "That of wands, the bludgeon of my power. Of coins, in the state coffers. Of cups, in which to serve traitors gall and vinegar. Of swords, to cut off their heads." But, even more so, that which galvanizes the dictator's energy is the "all-consuming worship of the solitary vice that is power, a palpable and personal thing," like the glass marble that the patriarch rolls around in his palm. "And if you take this away from me, what will I be? What will I still have left?" asks Alejo Carpentier's *caudillo*.

Opposite:
The presidential family
as seen by the
Colombian painter
Fernando Botero, 1967.

Overleaf:
Providing healthcare and
food, Mexican soldaderas
followed the revolutionary
army everywhere,
not hesitating
to fight if necessary.
Photograph from 1911.

160

“The rule of conduct of *Señor Presidente*
is to never give anyone hope, to trample
them all, to punish them all, simply
because... The one who keeps his job
is there because he does what he is told.”

AUGUSTO ROA BASTOS

Rome, that Bolívar swore to liberate Latin America: "I swear before you, my master, I swear before the God of the fathers, I swear by them, I swear by my honor that I will not let my arm or soul rest until I have broken the chains that oppress us because of the will of Spanish government."

Bolívar, *El Libertador*, followed in the footsteps of the conquistadors, collecting on this path those whom the Spanish had enslaved, raising man at the same time as he roused men. Step by step—"the step that you had directed in advance," he wrote to Rodríguez; speech by speech—"you trained my heart to love justice, liberty and all that is great and beautiful"; alternating resounding victories and bloody defeats— "the art of victory is learned as part of the art of defeat." Without distinction of skin color or class, he attempted to give to all the people of Latin America the means of assuring their liberty gradually throughout their liberation. "Liberty like the independence of the earth, liberty like the refusal of slavery, liberty like the natural expansion of the dignity of man, liberty like a means of recovering social justice and democracy," wrote German Arciniegas. Fifteen years of unrelenting struggle, of exhausting campaigns—"I feel the energy of my soul increase and rise in the face of the magnitude of the perils." With giant steps, those of a "titan" wrote Rubén Darío, Bolívar, after having been around the world more than twice on horseback—the tough *llaneros* nicknamed him "iron-seat"—liberated an empire five times larger than Europe. After he arrived in Pucara, a small Indian town in southern Peru, close to Lake Titicaca, one of the rare Indian notables, José Domingo Choquehuanca, greeted him with the words that oral tradition has transmitted to the future: "Nothing that was done before was like what you have done. In order for us to be able to imitate you, there would have to be another world to liberate." Four years later, in July 1830, the Parisian revolutionaries of the Trois Glorieuses took the Hôtel de Ville, demanding a Republic "whose sacred fire had sprung up around Bolívar." Byron christened with his name the yacht that would take him to die for the liberty of Greece. As La Fayette wrote to him, liberal Europe had its eyes riveted to his life. And "to look into his life," said José Martí, "was to feel one's thought ringed in gold." To look into his life, read his letters, biographies and, especially the wonderful work by Gilette Saurat, or Gabriel García Marquez's *The General in His Labyrinth*, which recreated the hero in all his humanity, is effectively to dive into the joys that are full of the intelligence and ardor of Bolívar, an intelligence that escapes all constraints and diagrams, an ardor that led him to proclaim himself the lover of liberty and to maintain that "friendship is my passion," to speak of affection and love in his political letters.

Myths are made of images, and Bolívar's album is full of them, which are even more beautiful because they are real: the image of *El Libertador* in thigh-boots on his white horse entering liberated cities to the cheers of the crowd, his lean form wrapped in a blue tunic embroidered with gold. That of the seducer whom neither men nor women could resist: slim body, fine features and olive skin. Bolívar had a little bit of mixed blood, curly, flamboyant dark hair and radiant teeth and smile. That

Allegory painted on a shield in the honor of Simón Bolívar.

of a fraternal comrade, escorting and supporting his army as much as leading it, a soldier among soldiers, sharing their worst living conditions and tasks. That of a man of the world who is cultivated, refined and always demanding a well-laid table, with an impeccable bearing and a visible dignity of being. That of the fierce combatant who never admitted defeat and who, exhausted and destitute after bitter defeats, answered without hesitating whenever anyone asked him what he planned to do: "Triumph!" That of the magnanimous victor who was fair: "the real warrior derived his glory from defeating his enemies, not from destroying them." That of the spirited lover writing impetuous love letters between battles but maintaining that during the day he preferred the company of a philosopher, his master Rodríguez, to that of the most beautiful woman. That of a scrupulously decent, unselfish, generous man who distributed his fortune, then his revenues, to the point of dying in absolute destitution. That of the solitary hero, all skin and bone under his white linen suit, dying on his hammock, burning with fever, consumed by treachery and the crimes of the future tyrants of Latin America, forgiving in the name of unity but dying in a state of lucidity: "He who serves a revolution plows the sea." Images of Simón Bolívar, "Out of that prince of liberty, appeared—radiant—the real man," said José Martí.

Undoubtedly only the searing intensity of poets could perceive the elusive Bolívar—too well rounded a personality, too complete and so, too complex. As complex as the reality of the continent whose every contradiction he was aware of, that he embraced, that he righted by the blade of his sword, that he dissected with the precision of a scientist and analyzed with the prescience of a visionary. His spiritual nourishment consisted of the writings of Las Casas, Montesquieu, Rousseau, Voltaire and Spinoza, whom he could quote from memory. Bolivar copied from no model, but followed the precepts of Rodríguez, to whom he said he owed everything. He was constantly improvising, aware that universal principles could only be embodied in the distinctive characteristics of Latin America. "Never has the soul of a continent so completely permeated the soul of a man," said Martí. Bolívar was anything but a Utopian: he was surprising because he was always ahead of his times, there where changing reality challenged him, a reality that, braced by unshakeable ethics, he mastered with the sureness of a chess champion. From this reality he extracted the forms of action that would make the most advantageous use of it. He had no illusions about his fellow men, and only addressed the best among them. The thousand or so letters he left, spiced with his frankness about politics and a biting sense of humor, whose interpretation took his prey by surprise and clashed with the routine hypocrisy, bear witness to his constant clear-sightedness. Bolívar was fully aware of the contradiction between the facts, the social situation and the economic and moral disorder fostered by the Spanish colonizers, in whose opinion, in the words of Charles IV, "An American has no need to know how to read; it suffices for him to worship God and his representative, the King of Spain." He was aware of the threat from the north, the danger from those United States "that seem destined to spread misery throughout the Americas in the name of freedom." He taunted their "arithmetical spirit." A hundred years before the creation of the League of Nations, the institution that preceded the United Nations, he laid the foundations of the Pan American Union, "the supreme authority that would play the role of council in case of conflict, of a meeting place from which common dangers could be faced, of a faithful interpreter of public treaties and of a conciliator in case of disagreements." He brought into being a Latin American conscience, hitherto nonexistent, and his intention was to forge it through the only means possible: the education that would produce the new man. "Let us work so that love brings together the children of the continent of Columbus in a universal bond, and root out hatred, revenge and war from their midst." Guevara took this concept as his heritage.

But Latin America was not as mature as its *Libertador*. Although the continent followed him to war, it abandoned him in peace. The land of the prophet of Latin America, where he was adulated and shouted down, respected and humiliated, betrayed by the very people he had pardoned, soon proved to be too small for him —"let us leave, let us leave, we are no longer wanted in this land. . . ." Throughout the continent, at each anniversary of his birth, July 24, 1783, and his death, December 17, 1830, homage is paid to him. Everyone attempts to seize hold of his remains; everyone wants a share to satisfy those on his side. These small commemorative betrayals are merely the extension of the betrayals of the contemporaries of Bolívar, whose unifying project was sacrificed to struggles between factions and regions, to personal ambition, to the shortsightedness of everyday pettiness. Thus it goes for all great men.

Zapata, the Man of the People

Opposite:
Portrait of Simón Bolívar in
Lima by José Gil de Castro.

Page 175: Portrait of Zap-
ata, anonymous. On
November 11, 1915—two
years before the Bolshevik
Revlution—Zapata made
public his project for the
partial privatization of
large properties.

The oversized straw sombrero with its upturned rim, the long, bushy mustache, the black scarf knotted high around his neck, the cartridge belt slung across his shoulder—these four features call up his immediately recognizable image, identical to that of his people. Zapata the peasant, Zapata the Mexican, Zapata the rebel. A comic strip cliché? The stature of Emiliano Zapata is enough to shatter any caricature. "They buried Zapata in the depths of the earth, so much did they fear he would rise again to continue the struggle," says a Mexican *corrido*, a song. From beneath the outrageous proportions of the hat that hid his eyes when he lowered his head, his stare never yielded. He gazes out unmistakably, his eyes piercing through one timeless photograph after another. The look in his eyes is tangible, even when, in profile, his pupils cannot be seen. In the rare portraits or group photographs, among the partisans, next to Pancho Villa, politicians and transitory presidents, this fixed, obsessing stare is imperious. It is filled with a humanity that can make no concessions, for it has been dispossessed of every-

"I will never be anything but the prisoner of freedom and the future."

SIMON BOLIVAR

thing except itself. Burning yet melancholy, nurtured passionately on the earth from which his very being was molded: the Indian land. The Indian peasants who rose in their masses in response to his call themselves said they marched "glued to Zapata's horse's tail."

Top:
Zapata in 1914.
Bottom:
Demonstration of landless
peasants in Brazil, 1997.
Tens of thousands of
Brazilian families live in
encampments along
the highways in
various parts of the
country. Conditions of life are
very rudimentary.

He was one of them, barely better off than the poorest among them, a sharecropper who also had a parcel of land and a few head of cattle, in that fertile state of Morelos in the south of Mexico, where most were peons despoiled of their possessions and overexploited by the large sugar-producing haciendas established on their ancestral lands. In 1909, under the corrupt dictatorship of the elderly Porfirio Díaz, who had been in power for 33 years, when the last pieces of tribal land still in their hands were threatened by the greed of the *hacendados*, the peasants of Anenecuilco, the village where he was born, elected this calm man, just turned thirty, to lead their community. Born into a respected family, he was a man who could read and write, had learned to handle weapons when he had been press-ganged, and who had been up and down much of the country as a horse trainer in various haciendas. He could have grown rich, but realizing that in these luxurious stables the animals were far better treated than the *péons*, he returned, exasperated and clear-sighted, to share the fate of his people. On September 12, 1909, he was solemnly presented with the property deeds of this 700-year-old village, written in Nahuatl, that had been transmitted from one village chief to another for generations. From that day onwards, Zapata, who entrusted a friend with these documents, advising him never to risk his life lest he lose them, would unfailingly serve this land, synonymous with freedom and dignity. In the logical continuation of this commitment, he would carry out all his duties, including the duty to fight. Throughout the revolution that swept away the old dictator and shook Mexico for ten years, alone in the midst of intrigues, alliances, swings of loyalty, betrayals and bloody confrontations, Zapata would remain incorruptible, invincible and indestructible.

In the face of the terrible repression of those who followed the orders of Huerta, the dictator, he preached harmony, peace and fraternity with the rifles and canons of the Republic, and remained "the incarnation of patience and fertility, silence and hope, death and resurrection," as Octavio Paz later wrote. In 1911 he published his "Plan of Ayala," the manifesto of an agrarian revolution that would have to take place through the restitution of the land to the peasants, who had been bled white for too long by the *hacendados*. To this manifesto, the *hacendados* retorted that they should "sow seeds in their flower pots."

"Nearly all the programs and manifestos of

the revolutionary groups allude to the agrarian question," writes Octavio Paz in *The Labyrinth of Solitude*. "But only the Revolution of the South and its leader, Emiliano Zapata, set out the problem with clarity, decisiveness and simplicity."

Although his contemporaries knew deep in their hearts, as they admitted later, that Zapata had a clear understanding of the Mexican crisis and solutions to offer, their political spinelessness, personal ambitions and class interests, mingled with those of their big American neighbor, all worked against the acknowledgment of his vision.

Constantly betrayed by the political chiefs, slandered, dragged in the mud, insulted by everyone, Zapata used his unshakable moral strength against the bloody legend of him as the Attila of the South, concocted by those who, even after his death, remained powerless to conquer him, to bend him or to compromise his reputation. When he made his call, an army of peasants rose up. They would never betray him. Unlike Pancho Villa, the Centaur of the North, Zapata imposed harsh discipline on his soldiers, forbade pillage and destruction, punished robbery and pardoned the simple soldiers he took prisoner. For the most part, they chose to follow him. When he made his triumphant entry into Mexico City, alongside Villa, the city dwellers, terrified by the propaganda that had been spread, were expecting the worst from the "blood-thirsty, barbaric bandit." Following him, wearing their traditional white cotton clothes, the exhausted, starving men of his movement knocked politely on the doors of the bourgeois houses asking for food. These peasant soldiers, who, like their leader, never wore military uniforms, returned to their lands as soon as they could. The aim of Zapata, his constant preoccupation, was not to lead his men to war but to peace, a peace that respected their rights. "Reform, justice, freedom and law" was the leitmotif of the Zapatist movement right to the end. He had remarkable organizational abilities, and took advantage of even the briefest lull to implement his program. Octavio Paz points out "the profound historical conscience of this man, isolated amid his people and his race," and adds that his program, which "involved the liquidation of feudalism and the institution of laws at last adapted to the reality of Mexico" showed the way to the foundation of contemporary Mexico and to the reforms that President Lazaro Cardenas accomplished between 1934 and 1940.

In 1915, in the temporarily liberated state of Morelos, genuine agrarian reforms based on Indian tradition were applied straight away. The Zapatists were joined by young technicians and intellectuals from the anarchist unions, and succeeded, both politically and economically, in their first attempt to implement direct, self-managed democracy "in line with the habits and customs of each village." Zapata, the cult leader, had created the least personality-oriented movement in all Mexican history. His unbeaten guerilla tactics, his victories, his unbelievable resistance, the perfect cohesion of the Zapatist movement, the loyalty of his chiefs and his troupes all combined to make him the man who had to

Overleaf:
The people armed, detail from a mural by David Alfaro Siquieros entitled Emiliano Zapata's Agrarian Revolution. *National Museum of History, Chapultepec, Mexico.*

Opposite:
Mexican horsemen during the revolution (1910-1920).

178

"Sweet-smelling poppy of the Guerrero woods, never again will you see the great guerillero... Bouncing brook, what did that red carnation say to you? It said that the leader is not dead. Zapata will return to us."

MEXICAN *CORRIDO*

On January 1, 1994,
the Indians of Chiapas rose
to the cry of "land and freedom,"
proclaiming themselves Zapatistas.

be destroyed. The dispenser of justice, a slow-speaking man of few words, finally fell in 1919, victim of the traitors of Venustiano Carranza. On April 10, he took up the invitation of a general who had declared himself to be a dissident, saying he wanted to join forces with Zapata. At the gate of the hacienda where the meeting was to take place, a guard of honor presented arms. As the last note of the bugle died out, just when he was going through the gate followed by an escort of ten companions, the soldiers fired.

"Sweet-smelling poppy of the Guerrero woods, never again will you see the great guerillero . . . . Bouncing brook, what did that red carnation say to you? It said that the leader is not dead. Zapata will return to us."

Che Guevara, the *Condottiere*

Overleaf, left: Village of Kami, Bolivia, 1986. Right: Young Sandinista supporter demonstrating in Nicaragua.

Opposite: Che T-shirt with the slogan: "Be realistic, demand the impossible."

Below: Alberto Korda took the famous photograph of Ernesto Guevara on March 5, 1960 during a ceremony in honor of the victims of the sabotage in Cuban waters of the French ship La Coubre.

His image has gone round the world, and is still in orbit on the T-shirts of youth worldwide who barely know whose picture they display on their torso. From Paris to Bombay, from New York to Dakar, his effigy has become yet another commodity in souvenir shops, on the shelves with Eiffel Towers, Statues of Liberty and other *bric-à-brac*. In Cuba, Fidel, his friend, has put it onto key rings, paperweights and rum tumblers.

The photo that shows him staring at the horizon of his dreams, his eyes passionate from beneath his starred beret, is the most widely sold document in the world, the one most often reproduced. Although he seems to have posed for immortal posterity, does anyone know that this photo was taken by chance? He was in the second row at an official event. Alberto Korda, Castro's official photographer, was busy taking pictures when something drew his attention. He lifted his lens and discovered the almost absent stare, already looking elsewhere, drawn to new challenges. Without taking the time to frame his subject, sensing the urgency, the photographer clicked three, four times. At the time there were priorities other than protecting the ownership of a photo. Reproduced an infinity of times, the picture should have made Korda's fortune. It was never copyrighted, but he regretted nothing, for sometimes a chance occurrence puts things right.

The man known as "Che"—because he was from Argentina and was in the habit of thus addressing those to whom he spoke—cannot be

CHÉ
seamos realistas,
exijamos lo
imposibi!

"Give a thought once in a while to this *condottiere* of the 20th century."

ERNESTO CHE GUEVARA

discovered in the images we have of him. Each one of the rare photographs seems to correspond to a custom-made stereotype: a romantic hero possessing stunning beauty that was of no importance to him; the *guerillero* with a heart of gold; the Robin Hood with unfailing courage, the betrayed fighter whose emaciated face and bullet-ridden body lying on a school table in the Bolivian countryside are reminiscent of Mantegna's painting of Christ. But Guevara's charisma goes beyond this, inscribed in the unique truth about him—it is the truth of a human being, never too human, who thought that anything was possible if one had the will—particularly the happiness of peoples. This was a new idea in Latin America.

"Even though he may appear ridiculous," Guevara would say, "the true *guerillero* is guided by generosity." As a young student of medicine, he had traveled the length and breadth of the continent, his conscience and heart open all the while. Everywhere he found poverty, injustice, humiliation and terror. This experience was enough to make him decide, after just one night of discussion with Fidel Castro, to board the *Granma* with eighty-two men who were going to liberate Cuba from the tyranny of Batista—he was to be the doctor for the expedition. Just a few days later: baptism by fire. Of lying wounded in a sugar cane field, under in the Caribbean sun, he later wrote in his diary, "Immediately, I began thinking of the best way to die at that moment, when all appeared to be lost. I remembered a short story by Jack London, in which the protagonist, leaning on the trunk of a tree, prepares to end his life with dignity, knowing that he was condemned to freeze to death in the icy regions of Alaska." The doctor was thus forced to become a *guerillero*. In the opinion of Guevara, this meant being an ascetic in the knightly sense of Don Quixote. "Once more I feel the ribs of Rocinante at my heels. I'm on the road again with my shield at my side," he wrote to his parents before leaving for Bolivia. "Today, my willpower that I have polished with an artist's delight, which I've sharpened with the delight that an artist feels, will sustain my shaky legs and my weary lungs." As he took on increasing responsibility, Ernesto Guevara became Che, a man who acted as he thought, true to his convictions. His last letter, a will for his children, holds a formula that is so simple and pure it takes mankind a step forward: "Be always capable of feeling, in the depths of your heart, any injustice committed against anyone anywhere in the world."

Overleaf, left:
Installation by a Cuban
artist for a cultural
conference in Havana, 1968.
Right:
Anti-Pinochet
demonstration,
Santiago, 1983.

Opposite:
Ernesto Guevara
and Aleida March
entering Santa Clara,
December 30, 1958.

186

Felix, nicknamed "la Doña"—the great lady—who always refused to speak a word of English or to film in Hollywood, claimed an authentic Mexicanness that incorporated dignity, modesty, suppressed passion and sensitivity. By turns farm woman, peasant woman, revolutionary woman soldier, stunning dancer—she played "La Belle Otero"—Maria Felix exhausted the repertoire of heroines in Mexican cinema. For Europe she was simply La Belle Mexicaine, who was to become Lola de Castro, La Belle Abbesse of Jean Renoir's *French Cancan*, and the proud Ines Rojas of *La Fievre monta a El Pao*, by Luis Buñuel.

In his play *Orchids in the Moonlight*, Carlos Fuentes presents this insoluble antagonism between the Hollywood image and the authentic image in a cruel dialogue between two aging rivals who confront each other, indissolubly linked: Dolores del Rio and Maria Felix.

Evita

In all of Latin America, only one other woman has aroused an emotion, devotion and faith comparable to those awakened by the Virgin of Guadalupe. In many homes, the image of Evita is on the wall next to the Virgin. As in the case of the Morena, it is not about the materialization of life as flesh nor the absence created by death. Placed beyond time and matter by the love of the living, they walk above the crowds carried by their trembling. They exist in all their presence, not perceived by reason but instead simply felt.

"*Se siente, se siente, Evita esta presente,*" chanted the crowds of all ages gathered at the big demonstrations. "We feel it, we feel it, Evita is present." They were not necessarily only Peronists; that is another story. In Argentina there are several Peronisms, but only one Eva—Eva of the people. Like a current, like a talisman, the name comes from all the voices to form but one--an invincible energy.

"Era rubia y sus ojos celestes reflejaban la gloria del dìa," went the waltz of Blomberg and Maciel, a masterpiece of popular lyrics. Eva was blond, as blond as the Morena was brunette, as blond as the Negros, Cholos and Indios were black of hair and brown of skin—workers and peasants who came from the huge country that the *porteños*, the inhabitants of the port of Buenos Aires, called by a disdainful euphemism, "the Interior." "She was blonde and in her eyes the color of the sky was reflected the glory of the day." Eva had brown eyes, and doubtless she tinted her hair to look like the stars of North America when, still a young and poor provincial girl, she dreamt of being an actress. But when she became the Madonna of the Descamisados—the Peronists—her blondeness, her whiteness, the elegance and magnificence of her outfits and her jewels were the richness and dignity, the revenge and the pride, the resplendent glory of the *cabezas negras*, rogues of the Interior. Let us make no mistake here, malicious gossip and cheap films could change nothing; it is for them that she dressed in fairy tale dresses, they who truimphed with her when, adorned like an icon, she eclipsed all those

Overleaf, left:
Carmen Miranda, "the Brazilian bombshell" in the Busby Berkely musical The Gang's All Here, *1943.*
Right:
The Mexican actress Dolores Del Rio en 1929 in Edwin Carewe's Evangeline, *1929*

Opposite:
Eva Peron.

194

66 Everything is melodramatic
in the lives of the humble.
Because the poor don't invent
sorrow, they bear it.99

EVA PERON

"Why would I want feet since I have wings to fly?"

FRIDA KAHLO

"A pinned butterfly, frozen in flight," as the painter Ignacio Aguirre described her, "nailed with flowers," said the poet Carlos Pellicer, "leading my life encircled by steel," as Frida confided in her *Diary*. She would live life trapped between the pain of existence and a zest for life. Day after day, she made of herself a living self-portrait, a model from her canvasses that could return to them at any moment, like the Mayan monoliths that, as legend would have it, were enchanted gods. Of her prison of broken bones, she made a relic to which every day she erected an ardent chapel. Frida did not dress, she got into costume. Like Indian shamans donning the skin of a jaguar to take on its strength, she put on a second skin, violently alive, of traditional Mexico—a political as much as an aesthetic statement. She made her infirmity disappear under embroidered blouses and shawls, long skirts with flounces of lace, heavy jewelry, ribbons and flowers, metamorphosizing at will, unceasingly reconstructing her mutilated body. She who always said of herself "I am disintegration," also affirmed "Me, I have too many wings. Let them be cut and we will fly!" Wings once again the same as the mirror-hands of the Yai of Asturias: "My hands symbolize my absence. It is through them that I leave myself, what I am, what I think, what I feel, what I do, to multiply myself in other versions of me, which are like me and are only an image of this me that I am not . . . How many others! So many others! This one with the smiling face! That one with the serious expression! This one who is about to collapse into tears! That one with the thoughtful look, and this other which appears indifferent as if everything was the same to her!"

Frida Kahlo would appear, and each of her appearances was an incarnation, the incarnation of an invisible world, underground, where life and death were engaged in a merciless struggle from which neither would come out victorious. Our Lady of Suffering and Our Lady of the Resurrection, Frida Kahlo was the opposite of a *mater dolorosa*, she was the armor-plated angel unceasingly defying the dragon and suffering. Recounting his meeting with the Mexican artist at a concert given at the Fine Arts Museum, Carlos Fuentes wrote: "It was the entrance of an Aztec goddess, the mother-goddess, draped in her skirt of snakeskin, displaying her lacerated and bleeding hands like other women would sport a brooch. Or was it Tlazolteotl, the goddess of both purity and impurity, at the Indian pantheon, the female vulture who must feed on waste matter to purify the world. But perhaps we were looking at the Spanish Earth Mother, the Lady of Elche, rooted to the earth by her heavy helmet of stone, her earrings of cartwheels, her pectorals displacing her breasts, rings transforming her breasts into birds' claws." She wrote in her *Diary*, not long before her death: "We are going towards ourselves, through millions of stone beings, bird creatures, astral creatures, microscopic beings, beings that are the source of ourselves."

Overleaf, left:
Portrait of Frida Kahlo by
Nickolas Maray.
Right: Frida Kahlo and Leon
Trotsky during his exile in
Mexico, 1937.

Opposite:
Frida Kahlo and Nickolas
Maray, circa 1939.

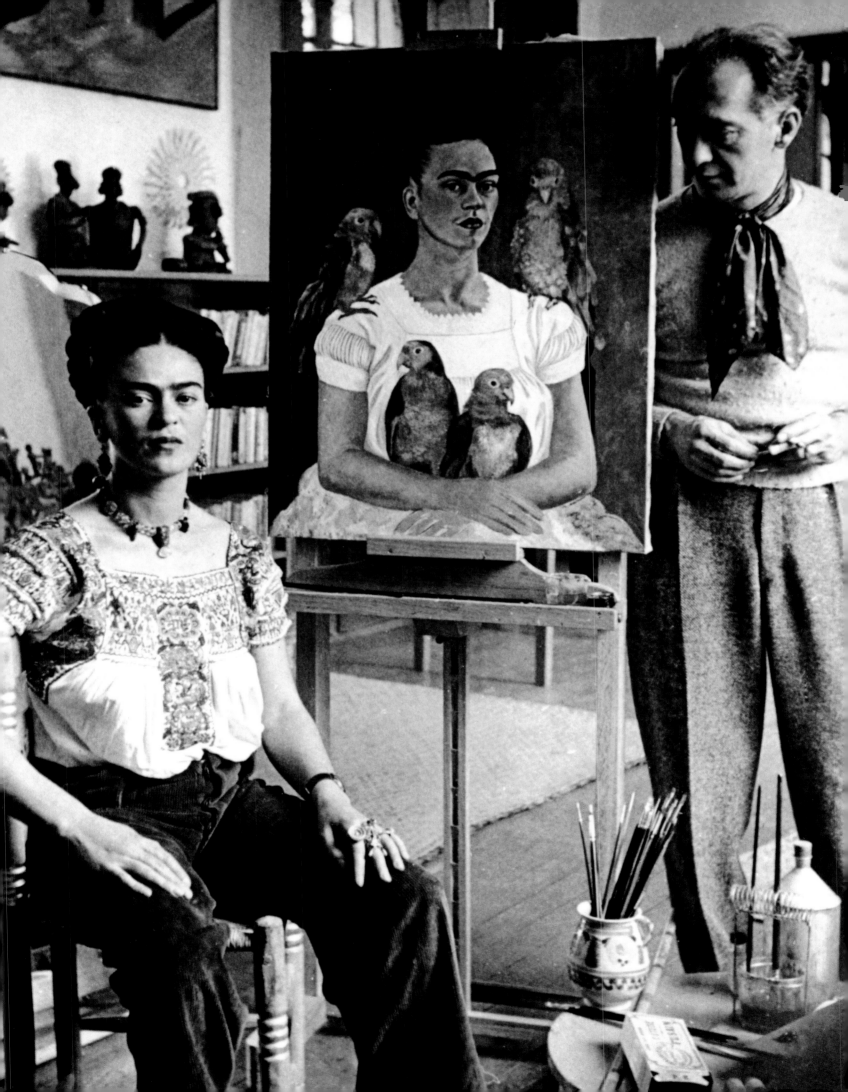

CHAPTER IX

THE CITIES

From the founding of Mexico by Hernán Cortés to that of Brasilia by President Juscelino Kubitschek, the capitals of Latin America have sprung up from nothing, like so many dreams of order and accord. A social order translated into an esthetic harmony, its criteria evolved as a result of the great political and economic upheavals, but always served the designs of those in power. The colonial metropolis—emblem and instrument of territorial, political and religious domination, whose jurisdiction extended over vast regions—was carefully planned out through successive laws and rulings. From Havana to Buenos Aires, through Caracas, Bogotá, Lima, La Paz, Quito and Santiago, the urban layout always resembled the same checkerboard, as straight as a ruler. The impressive regularity was rarely broken by any unavoidable natural obstacle. A checker board made up of *manzanas*, square or rectangular groups of houses forming *cuadras*, blocks of equal dimensions cut across by four roads and opening onto a limitless space, allowed at one time a balanced expansion of the town. At the same time the navel, heart and brain of the colonial project, the Plaza de Armas, Plaza Real or Plaza Mayor was the formal expression of the administrative supervision exercised by the Crown. It was around this square—an open space lined with arcades—that the checkerboard was arranged and towards which all activities converged. The square was surrounded by the tall buildings of the cathedral, government headquarters, *Cabildo* or town hall, bishops' palace, treasury, court and prison.

In the center, the open space where the morning market was held served also as a stage for the continual productions put on by colonial power, which culminated in the baroque excesses of the 18th century.

Military parades and religious processions, large civil celebrations to mark aristocratic marriages or funerals, executions and *corridas*—all of these took place in the Plaza Mayor, around which both the reality and the spectacle of the abduction of souls and economic pillage were centered. Exclusively White, an urban hierarchy was built around it that corresponded to the colonial social order.. It was from this center, heavy with symbolism, that the allocation of residential property was organized—in tiers according to degree of mixed blood, the Indians being left on the outskirts. The domes and bell towers of churches and convents marked out the different districts. Invariably repeated and reproduced down to the scale of small provincial towns, the ruling capital covered the continent in a maze of mirrors that reflected everywhere the dazzling and suffocating splendr of the Spanish Crown's unending power.

Up until independence, the history of Latin America was acted out in the Plaza Mayor and was mixed up with the history of the vice-royal and provincial capitals. Spanish colonialism was succeeded by the neocolonialism of a Creole oligarchy, which, in the name of trade liberalization, enriched itself significantly by delivering the continent's resources and collaborating, in the positivist euphoria of industrial progress, in setting up sustainable underdevelopment. As evidence of its integration into modernity, this same oligarchy, with its eye turned towards London and Paris, transformed the appearance of the colonial capital by importing Haussmannian architecture. The architects and engineers, landscapers and sculptors who constructed and decorated the new buildings of power were principally French and Italians. A branch of the great European bourgoisie, the Latin American capital thus acquired a "civilizing" mission against the barbarity that was symbolized by the farmer—the Indian—considered uneducated and behind the times. The Plaza de Armas, which had become the Plaza de la Independencia, went from being functional to monumental—as theatrical as the showiness of the colonial baroque period. Replaced by a garden with a bandstand, the market moved further away to be held in a covered structure inspired by the pavilions of Victor Baltard. Although the layout of the colonial square was respected in the Andean capitals such as Quito and Lima, there was no trace of it in the great burgeoning ports such as Rio de Janeiro, Buenos Aires, Montevideo and Santiago. Surrounding the square, everywhere wide avenues opened up—clearings in a city modeled on the Champs Élysées, lined with trees and

*Overleaf, left:
Map of the city of
Tenochtitlan.
Illustration from a
letter from Cortés to Emperor
Charles V in 1524.*

*Bottom and opposite:
Center of Quito, Ecuador.
Some blocks of the colonial
city center are now classified
UNESCO landmarks.*

208

66 Of all the arts, architecture has made
the most progress in Colombia,
its successes all the more surprising
as it had no masters to guide it other
than books and stamps. **99**

MOLLIEN

cafés, and finished off at either end by equestrian statues of *Libertadors* and Indians, freethinkers leading the population, feathered replicas of the Républiques in Paris created by Auguste Rodin, Frédéric-Auguste Bartholdi and Antoine Bourdelle. With theaters, operas, libraries, fine art museums, banks, commercial arcades, shops selling foreign novelties and huge tea salons and jockey clubs in the pure English tradition, these beautiful neighborhoods became the exclusive district and showcase of an elite that affirmed its ties to the West by distancing itself, ostensibly, from all that might bring to mind a mixed culture. From now on, away from the center of the town, the new bourgeois residences took on the appearance of Swiss chalets, Italian or Moorish villas, Norman manor houses, or small chateaux of the Loire valley. Europe had dreamed of America; it was now America that dreamed of Europe and which, in an attempt to escape its reality, rejected its people as one tries to fend off a recurrent nightmare.

This segregation was also materialized through the construction of the first ring roads. These peripheral boulevards held back the laborers from the interior of the country, or those who disembarked from European or Chinese cargo boats. The first "shanty towns" thus made their appearance, soon increasing tenfold with the crisis of 1929, which provoked a drastic reduction in exports of cereals, meats and ores, and resulted in a rush of jobless farmers heading for the capital. Periods of crisis and pseudo-prosperity alternated with each other, as did populist and repressive governments, in keeping with the pressure from North America. But the gulf between the towns and countryside never stopped increasing. The large towns continued to bring together workshops, factories and depots and to benefit from certain investments, as well as health, social welfare and building infrastructures, which, as if by miracle, had escaped corruption and speculation.

Accelerated by the enormous demographic pressure, the urban hypertrophy generated what Octavio Paz rightly called "a cancerous development." The official town, which had become compact and vertical, bristling with concrete and neon, was crisscrossed by a network of motorways and interchanges and grew continously, imperceptibly. In the greatest anarchy, unofficial districts sprung up, sometimes overnight, on any available land next to rubbish depots or areas liable to flooding. In the mud and waste appeared labyrinths of hastily erected shacks, made of planks and a few bricks, bamboo or reeds, sheet metal, boxes and plastic. They had no water, no electricity, and were without sewer drainage—illegal towns, shored up by the despair of those with nothing more to lose. They displayed imagination, ingenuity, tenacity, solidarity and a sense of organization and self-management that was constantly evolving and took the municipal authorities by surprise. *Favelas* in Brazil, *barriadas* in Peru, *ranchitos* in Venezuela, *colonias proletarias* in Mexico, *villas miserias* in Argentina. Each country had a different name for what Pablo Neruda described as "the huge leprous slums . . . of houses as dark as rat holes . . . to the swarming degradation, to the accusatory gangrene. . . ." There, in the violence of promiscuity and the power of its vitality, survived the majority of "city dwellers" of Latin America.

Opposite:
Potosi, Bolivia. In the 17th century, this was the largest city in Latin America. Beginning in 1545, 30,000 tons of silver were mined in Cerro Rico where 6 million Indian and Africa slaves lost their lives.
Below:
Favela, Rio de Janeiro.

Buenos Aires

Closed in on itself between the ocean and the pampa—between two silences, two voids—an intermittent and fantastical city stretches out. What is Buenos Aires after all? The immense port has forgotten the sea behind the widest river in the world, the Rio de la Plata, with its red and motionless water. "He who has never listened to the voice of the river will never understand the sadness of Buenos Aires. It is the sadness of the silt calling for a soul!" exclaimed Adan Buenosayres, the hero in Leopoldo Marechal's book of the same name, a metaphysical odyssey set in the city of the 1920s. On the one side is the Plata, which projects across the city its "curtain of the sea and dreams," as Manuel Mujica Lainez wrote; on the other, the plain, which begins in the dusty roads of the suburbs and ends at the end of the earth, at the bottom of the map, symmetrical witchcraft around the margins of water and earth. Does Buenos Aires take pride in possessing the longest roads in the world, and among them, the longest—Rivadavia, which cuts the city in two "half for the river and half for the pampa"? The city is so huge that for Borges it is "a transcription of the plain, whose exhausted equilibrium continues in the straightness of the roads and houses." The roads are "long like expectation," opening out onto the sky, cut across by other roads, also parallel or perpendicular. One can travel along them for ages without ever approaching the end. The vanishing point is always the same, the two sides having the same full and hypnotic intensity, which roams around the city like a mirage. Four infinities meet at each crossroads." Buenos Aires comes from elsewhere—From Paris and Madrid, from Naples and London, from Smyrna, Kiev and Warsaw. It is a city of lost steps, open to those who leave for the furthest-away points, as if attending to the most important things first.

Top:
Bar in Plaza Dorrega, in the San Telmo district of Buenos Aires, where the tango was born.
Bottom:
At the back of the collectivos, the buses of Buenos Aires, titles of tangos bloom.

Opposite:
Avenue Corrientes in Buenos Aires, the Argentinean Broadway.

Buenos Aires was for millions of immigrants the port of last chance, gathering on its banks "the social backwash of a hundred nations." Buenos Aires—World's End—exiled to the ends of the earth, an arch detached from all the continents, run aground on nostalgia, a nostalgia that sticks to the city like a lining of the soul, woven by each solitude of as much hope as regret. The city itself is constructed of bits of Europe—Madrid squares, French stations and cemeteries, London or Milanese avenues. But Buenos Aires cannot be discovered; it must be deciphered. Step by step, dream by dream, in each destiny, in the light of memory and the twilight of melancholy, with, wrote Cortazar, "the secret and admirable despair with which we have invented everything."

❝ The sadness of Corrientes Street where illusions hang on, sad because it is ours. ❞

HOMERO EXPOSITO (TANGO)

The best moment to attempt to tame it is in "the hour when everything becomes part of a deeper, enigmatic existence . . . A mysterious occurrence takes place: the day draws to a close and night begins," wrote Ernesto Sabato, with a single untranslatable word to unite these two expressions at once: *anochece*. It is through many afternoons that the city gradually enters into us," noted Borges. In the imprecise city, behind dull blue-green net curtains are illuminated watertight, closed places, floating in a green light: the cafés of Buenos Aires—schools of all things. In the large and gloomy parks, in the squares, in the gardens and court-yards, alone, in couples, or in small groups, one can savor the bitter jubilation of being *porteño*—another untranslatable word, the closest definition of which would be "a man who descends from the port," "a man alone, in expectation," according to the title of Raul Scalabrini Orti's book. In this "manual of the solitary porteño," as Sabato called it, Scalabrini Ortiz analyzes the condition of being in Buenos Aires as a fluctuation in oneself that follows the drift of the uncertain. The *porteño* does not walk, he does not run; he strolls, he wanders, he saunters, and "the life of the city carries on aimlessly, tossed about between events that slip through the net of the best prophecy." To tame Buenos Aires, it is necessary to spend hours listening to this expectation until dreams can be seen circulating and endeavors crossing over one another.

"What is Buenos Aires then?" asked Borges, " a secret, invisible city; we can share it but we cannot communicate it to others." "Only sometimes Buenos Aires gives itself over to its inhabitants, when one approaches it from dreams and memories, when one possesses it armed with imagination and myth," revealed Cortazar in *Buenos Aires Buenos Aires*. In order to penetrate the mystery of this mythological city, oscillating on the boundaries of the real world, conservative writers and popular poets have, from generation to generation, shuffled and reshuffled the same words, the same images, like so many cards tirelessly aligned in all directions to reach an unlikely conclusion. The odor of jasmine, of flower-ing honeysuckle and the perfume of grass that smells of pampa and legend, the creaking gate and the narrow passage that lead to the sweetness of the patio of the low houses—the vague terrain where childhoods are lived out—the impasse, the ditch and the embankment, the paving stones crossed by the tracks of former tramways, the Alsina bridge with its look of the Great Wall of China, the grocery store lit up at night, the glimmer of the streetlight, a dog howling at the moon, love hidden beneath a doorway, the lament of the *bandonéon* in the starry evening—"South, a wall and beyond."

Buenos Aires is breathed in through its districts and suburbs, barrios and arrabales, in the sacred silt of the arrabal, as Marechal wrote. "Each one of us," said Borges, "has told of his small part of the suburbs, but no one has told the whole story." Fleeting images are, barely glimpsed, yet already erased. Every-thing takes place on street corners—angles with cut-off corners—where pale pink walls, "like the back of a card" present the invariable setting of the tango and

Opposite:
The port of Buenos Aires,
La Boca, is the working-class
neighborhood where immi-
grants from Europe—mostly
from Italy—arrived a century
ago. At the time the tango
was danced in brothels.

The enchantment of the unmoving river,
of "the muddy and daydreaming Plata,"
which projects onto the city its "curtain of sea
and chimera," as Manuel Mujica Laines wrote
in his *Song to Buenos Aires*, is echoed by that plain,
which begins in the dusty streets of the suburbs
and ends where the world ends,
on the bottom of the map of the world.

of life, of myths and history, and no one knows if the tango dreamed up Buenos Aires or vice versa. Does it still exist, has it ever existed? Nothing of what makes the soul of Buenos Aires is immediately visible, immediately readable, and it is not by chance that the great writers of the city are also great translators. Equivalences, superimpositions, circles and labyrinths are traced around the city by these men who tracked the soul of the city on every street corner. Buenos Aires is an insomniac city—does it really exist beyond those who, in order to live there, reinvent it night after night? Perhaps one cannot really live in Buenos Aires, for it is the city that lives in us and even grabs us and haunts us like the presence of an absence never filled. "Buenos Aires," said Borges, "is the other road, the one on which I have never walked."

Mexico City

"The pulverized shit of three million human beings without latrines. The powdered excrement of 10 million animals that defecate in the road. Eleven million tons of chemical waste per day. The lethal exhaust of three million engines . . . and all this at an altitude of 2,300 meters, compressed under a layer of icy air and surrounded by a circular wall of mountains: trapped waste." This was Mexico City, the largest city in the world, as described by one of its most famous writers, Carlos Fuentes.

Mexico D.F., with 30 million inhabitants, a megalopolis invisible through a fog of noxious pollution. *Mexico toxico*: toxic Mexico. Between factory smoke and belching exhaust pipes, of the 5,000 squared kilometers of Federal Detritus—as it has been called by the punks playing on the initials of Federal District—burst forth snapshots of scenes, characters and wild gleaming images of a vitality as strong as the city is deadly. How is it possible to resist? "Leave the city before it's too late!" warns one advertisement for a garbage company. A city of 30 million inhabitants, and yet, each day the large bus stations pour out more than 1,000 new arrivals, thrown by the poverty of the countryside into the jaws of the screaming hydra. Some speak only *mixteque*, or *nahuatl*, and hardly any words of Spanish. Dignified, silent, lost, they descend from the Yellow Arrow or White Star coaches, sort out their identical bundles of belongings, count their chickens, goats and children, and leave in search of the much-awaited capital. In the hills, the shanty towns wait. Each year the toxic fumes of the contaminated city kill more than 100,000 children there. The bloodthirsty Huitzilpochtli did not ask time of his Aztec priests. In an instant of time, the Marias, immutable peasants from another time, light up a street corner abandoned to the frenzy of the impossible traffic with their embroidered blouses. Kneeling or squatting, oblivious to the chaos, they officiate, undaunted, at a secular altar where, on immaculate linen, fuschia watermelons, pink mangoes and orange papayas are offered on the bare ground. On their backs, protected by a *rebozo*, a shawl striped in the same tones as the

Opposite:
The City Awakens,
by the Argentinean painter
Antonio Segui,
who was born in 1934.

216

fruits, the inevitable baby is asleep. These are visions from the frescoes of Diego Rivera, José Clemente Orozco, David Alfaro Siqueiros, muralists of a militant beauty. The dream revealed on the walls of Mexico by the great revolutionary painters of the 1920s—of the reappropriation by the Indian masses of their own destiny—had not yet come to pass. The Marias only convey everyday images of underdevelopment, capturing a beauty in which can be found the modesty of a swan song. Only the custom of painting the town has survived, in a populist pictorial art that expresses suffering and desire with a naïve affection, and pokes fun at the urban madness with a humor whose caustic nature stands up to the pollution, the corruption and the constant violence of overcrowding. Every space, still or moving, is a stage for Mexico to act out its street theatre where its history, past and present, continually confronts itself. How could it be otherwise, when from the bowels of the city, opened up in the construction of the subway, sprung up, like a golem, the colossal monolith of Coatlicue, Aztec Goddess of the Earth?

A war of images and slogans, from which the Big Brother of the North does not necessarily come out winning, is carried out on the advertisement posters constantly turned round by avenging minds. Incarnated in the giant icons of wrestlers and supermen, virgins and vamps, devils and angels, skeletons and pin-ups, revolutionary leaders and Aztec emperors, their appearances accompanied by warnings, maxims and slogans, declarations of religious or political faith, loving or menacing messages. Having disappeared behind the thick brown cloud that covers the city, Popocatepetl reappears on the sides of trucks and coaches, taking on a reddish hue below its ruff of snow. The trucks and cars are covered by clusters of people, who, amidst the groaning of overheated engines and the clamor of triumphal radios, run the "made in mad Mexico" race along a stretch of avenues that are as broad as motorways, widening out at times to as many as fourteen lanes. A suffocating racket, to the rhythm of incessant horns, juke boxes blaring and loud televisions in all the cafés where, following the ups and downs of a football match, everyone shouts together with joy at a "gooooaal" or in anger at defeat. Planes circle overhead in the yellowish sky. The octopus, although it has lost its center, clasps tightly to the airport with its tentacles. An incredible snapshot of a crazy city, here lies "the most limpid region of the air."

According to Carlos Fuentes in *Burnt Water*, a book marking the turning point of Mexico the Mutant, Mexico was "a city full of tomorrows," where the air was so pure that at two o'clock in the morning "one could already breathe in the odor of the damp earth of the coming day, inhale the perfume of the jacarandas, and smell, close at hand, the volcanos." To the south of the city, in the former colonial villages of San Angel, San Jeronimo and Coyoacan, where Diego Rivera, Frida Kahlo, André Breton and Leon Trotsky once lived, and where today artists, intellectuals and students have taken refuge among the last remaining trees, one can still imagine "the roads of a city not like the one seen today—deformed and scrofulous, full of lumps of cement and hidden swellings—but small and made of pastel colors." Elsewhere, in the Plaza Garibaldi, in the shadow of the cathedral

Opposite:
Mexico City.

218

66 Oh, Ashley, let's run away, you and I.
We could go to Mexico . . .
and we could be so happy there. 99
Scarlett to Ashley in *Gone with the Wind*

and the last colonial residences built by Cortés with stones from temples and Aztec palaces, can be seen lined up one after the other the *cantinas*—cheap eating places with pink, mauve or green walls. Against this handkerchief of delicate color, shrunk away from the immense greyness, bursts forth the euphoria of guitars and trumpets, violins and powerful songs from a score of orchestras of mariachis playing all different kinds of rancheras on top of each other. The mariachi—in his shiny boots, black trousers with silver frog fastenings, a finely worked belt buckled over an impeccable shirt, a *lavaliere*—a loosely tied bow tie—made of bright silk, a bolero embroidered with silvered droplets, and his sombrero decorated like a birthday cake, his voice harsh yet moving beneath an imposing moustache—is a distillation of the Mexico of operetta. But there, where André Breton recognized surrealism in its pure state, one would not be proud of appearances. Although tourists are happy with the clichéd version of the mariachi, it is no less authentic—a musical nanny that consoles the *chilango*, so roughly treated by the city, against all ills. There was no celebration without mariachis and no Mexico without celebrations! To the sound of the mariachis, "the favored daughter of the Apocalypse," as Carlos Fuentes always called it, danced at the foot of its volcano until it became giddy. "We will go to Mexico and everything will be wonderful" said Scarlett to Ashley in *Gone With the Wind*.

Brasilia

The "capital of hope," as André Malraux called it, Brasilia, conceived of as a radically new socialization initiative as much as an urban project, brought with it a willingness to break with the colonial past and the existing neocolonialism. A myth of triumphant and liberating modernity, Brasilia was intentionally situated at the watershed between the basins of the Amazon, Plata, and São Francisco rivers, which went under the name of Lake El Dorado in old cartography and where, in the 19th century, Dom Bosco, patron saint of the Salesians, saw the Promised Land appear in a dream. Designed by Lucio Costa, and clearly visible from the sky, the huge white bird of so many dreams came to rest finally in 1960, at the heart of the country, "consecrating six million square kilometers of land to the general progress of Brazil," as declared President Juscelino Kubitschek. A town with a radiant and democratic future, an egalitarian city where, regardless of social position, all could benefit from "conditions of physical and moral safety appropriate for the harmonious development of human nature." A symbol, also, of a national autonomy was turning its back on Europe and opening up towards a collective pioneering

Below:
The Supreme Court, Brasilia, which was built between 1958 and 1960. It was designed by the architect Oscar Niemeyer.

Opposite:
Brasilia, the capital of Brazil.
The city was imagined by José Bonifácio in 1823 and dreamed of by Dom Bosco in 1883; its first stone was laid in 1922.

Overleaf:
Sao Paolo. The city has a population of 20 million and is Brazil's financial hub.

66 The thrilling and languid charm
of tropical nights when one
can die indifferently
for love and liberty. 99

ROBERT DESNOS

spirit, to the development of the rural interior of the country—a town that had emerged from the mud and dust in only four years, built shoulder to shoulder by Brazilians for Brazilians. Borne along by the musical architecture of Oscar Niemeyer—who, in designing the project, engaged his conviction of humanist communism, a sensibility involving curves and a lightness of choreography—Brasilia surprised and moved the whole world. But, for many reasons, the white bird of the dream never managed to fly, and Brasilia quickly became a capital of splendid solitude, of sterile boredom. Except in the satellite towns and favelas, which, from the arrival of the first construction workers, never cease to rebuild themselves!

Havana

First there is the Malecon, a barrage against the sea, "a double horizon of a wall and a band of blue—a fold that is the scar of the watershed." The curve of the Malecon is like a fragment of infinity, at the same time boustrophedon, palimpsest and palindrome: interminably traveled along in both directions, paced out, driven along, lived, relived, dreamed of and missed. A perpetual voyage where Havana both begins and ends. Untranslatable Malecon: is it a jetty? A boulevard? A quay? An avenue? A promenade? All of these things. Running the whole length of the town from one end to the other, a space wide enough for lovers' rendez-vous, children's games, sedate families, lonely sadness, defiant solidarity, night orchestras and phantoms in exile, there, on the other side, in Miami. The unceasingly surprising discovery of this sea just beyond the quay. On the other side from the surf, badly protected by the heavy parapet, "these old houses that have ended up by becoming another barrier of reefs, as a result of the saltpeter and the sea dew that clings to them when there is wind and waves on the days when the sea leaps across the road . . ." wrote Guillermo Cabrera Infante in *Three Trapped Tigers*, one of the masterpieces of contemporary literature. An oceanic Caribbean. And, above everything, the sky, changing like the sea, clear or full of clouds, with a calm sun in the morning that by the end of the day is raging, blazing and flaming. Havana has superb evenings and dawns that are like the beginning of time.

Like Venice or Lisbon, the town is constructed around water and light; the vertigo of the open sea is countered by a network of columns, railings, balustrades and corner irons. In a delightful little book dedicated to the subject, Alejo Carpentier calls it "The town of columns," with "forests of columns," whose tops made of grey stone mingle with the grey scales of the old palm trees. Assaulted by the tropics, the pavements palpitate and are pushed up by powerful roots. Everywhere, the former forest pushes up through the ground underfoot. Through all its veins, with all its vigor: jacarandas, flamboyant trees, palms and Cuban bay trees, built like shacks, with curtains of lianas falling from

Overleaf:
Rio de Janeiro (left)
and Acapulco
(right, a work
by Solange Galazzo, 2000)
by night.

Opposite:
Havana.

226

" **If I get lost,
look for me in Cuba.** "

FEDERICO GARCIA LORCA

them to the ground. Even the roads themselves—where the legendary American cars prowl, like wild cats ready to pounce—are not spared. On the facades of pistachio green, nougat pink and bright blue are porticos with porticos above them, and higher up, balconies with cornices, balustrades, volutes, arabesques, caryatids, baskets of fruits and flowers. Works appear to be made of minerals and vegetables, or is it the mimicry of wrought iron that proliferates everywhere? It is that, by many tricks, the town seeks to soothe "the being hounded by so much sun, more sun, and yet more sun." A merciless sun "that, at 10 o'clock in the morning burns like a fire and by midday becomes a veritable vertical flame-thrower," according to Cabrera Infante. To break up the "pulsating light," Havana invented the *medio punto*, a "huge fan of glass, whose multicolored rose windows were placed above the Persian windows and doors that were secretly closed. In the maze of the former aristocratic residences, now divided up, the *mamparas*—openwork interior partitions—took over, reflecting from room to room joy and sadness, anger and cheerfulness, hate and love. There was discussion over the method used and the draught where one can follow "the arrival of the fresh air," the place of freshness envisaged as the very heart of the rose of the winds. "There where one can smell, in certain months, the breeze from Cojimar" carrying over the door "its breath of far-off rains," the place where the rocking chair is positioned—like a little boat where, in the sweetness of tropical evenings, Cuban nonchalance rocks interminably. Havana is a town in perpetual motion. To the rhythm of inexhaustible conversations which follow, everywhere and in all tones, light and shade, stars and neon, air and heat, words and laughter, electric fans and car radios, songs and music, dance and love, "rum, bars, roses, and sailors." "Here are Whites, Blacks, Chinese, mulattos . . . The colors have run and not a single tone is stable," wrote Nicolas Guillen. Unremit-

Overleaf:
Taxi, Cuba.

Below:
Image from the film
I Am Cuba *by the Russian*
director Mikahil
Kalatozishvili, which
depicted the decadence
of Batista's regime.

Opposite:
Ernest Hemingway in Peru
during the shooting of
The Old Man and the Sea,
adapted from his book by
the director John Sturges
in 1958.

Overleaf:
Havana, between a mythical
past and present-day reality.

tingly, Havana moves and surprises with its joyous and always triumphal vigor. It was this that seduced the fiery Hemingway, in revolt against North American puritanism. Of this fantastic journey, which, from *mojito* to *daiquiri*, took him from the narrow streets of the old city to his lair of the Finca da Vigia, there remains today only a more or less fanciful itinerary, duly marked out, which day-trippers go around in half an hour. Would "Papa" Hemingway, as the Cubans affectionately called him, still claim to feel more happy as an American at El Floridita—one of his favorite bars—than in New York? Viewed from the terrace of his favorite hotel, the Ambos Mundos, as from the tops of the palaces built by the Mafia in the 1930s—used as film sets for musicals or Hollywood horror films—Havana takes on the appearance of Dresden after it was bombed. Bits of

collapsed walls and roofs reveal improbable staircases supported by thin air, networks of electric cables tangled up with washing lines, lifts with wardrobes and fridges with cupboards, mounds of rubble on top of which sit washing machines and bathtubs, skeletons of stone with flowers growing out of them, false ruins resuscitating matter and form in a continual recycling. Havana could have created Piranèse. From out of these buildings that are no more, so much that they appear to be ready to crumble, come always impeccably clean, smiling men and women, children in school uniforms with neatly parted hair and piles of books under their arms. The mysteries of dignity. From where comes, also, despite and because of everything, this impression of inalienable freedom, tolerance and gentleness that appears to be profoundly rooted in the soul of Havana, no matter what happens? Without doubt, as one of the first cities founded in Latin America, it has much to teach us. "First it was only a diffuse light like that which precedes the appearance of the moon; then the lights become fixed points . . . The old man kept course for these lights." Was this sentence from *The Old Man of the Sea*, written upon seeing this town for the first time, just a cryptic message?

Bibliography

General Works

Bernand Carmen, Gruzinski Serge, *Histoire du Nouveau Monde,* Paris, Fayard, 1993.

Buchet Martine, *Panama: A Legendary Hat*, New York , Assouline, 1996.

Cali François, *L'Art des conquistadors,* Geneva, Musée Barbier-Mueller, 1992.

Foucault, Michel, *The Order of Things*, New York, Vintage, 1970.

Galeano Eduardo, *Open Veins of Latin America: Five Centuries of The Pillage of The Continent*, Paris, Monthly Review Pr., 1998.

Le Clézio J.M.G, *Le Rêve mexicain*, Gallimard, 1988.

Prescott W.H., *Histoire de la conquête du Pérou*, Paris, Pygmalion, 1992.

Saurat Gilette, *Simón Bolívar le Libertador*, Paris, Grasset, 1990.

Toussaint-Samat Maguelone, *Histoire naturelle et morale de la nourriture*, Paris, Larousse, 1997.

Uslar Pietri Arturo, *Insurgés et Visonnaires d'Amérique Latine*, Paris, Critérion, 1995.

Wachtel Nathan, *La Vision des vaincus*, Gallimard, 1971.

Womack John Jr, *Zapata and Mexican Revolution*, New York, Knopf, 1969.

Terra Incognita, The Conquest of El Dorado

First images of America, The impact of the New World on the Old, Los Angeles, edited by Fredi Chiapelli Univ. of Calif. Press L.A., 1976, II vol.

Fabulas y leyendas de El Dorado, Barcelone, Ed. de Juan Gustavo Cobo Borda, Tusquets Circulo, coll. « Biblioteca del Nuevo Mundo », 1987.

Noticias secretas y publicas de America, Ed. de Emir Rodriguez Monegal, Tusquets Circulo, coll. « Biblioteca del Nuevo Mundo », 1984.

Ailly Pierre d', *Ymago Mundi*, Paris, Maisonneuve Frères, 1930.

de Las Casas Bartolomeo, *The Devastation of The Indies: A Brief Account,* Baltimore, Johns Hopkins University Press, 1992.

Diaz del Castillo Bernal, *The Conquest of New Spain,* New York, Viking Press, 1963; *The Discovery And Conquest of Mexico*, New York, De Capo Press, 1996.

Leon-Portilla Miguel, *Aztec Thought And Culture: A Study of The Ancient Nahuat I Mind*, University of Oklahoma Press, 1990.

Madariaga Salvador de, *El auge y el ocaso del imperio español en América*, Buenos Aires, Espasa-Calpe, 1977.

Reichel-Dolmatoff Gerardo, *Orfebreria y chamanismo*, Medellin, Colina, 1990.

Sahagun Bernardino de, *Historia natural de las Indias*, Ed. Porrua.

Poetry and fiction

Alegria Ciro, *Novelas Completas*, Peru, A. del Hoyo, 1963.

Amado Jorge, *Gabriela, Glove And Cinnamon*, Bard Books, 1998 ; *Cacau,* Rio de Janeiro, Record, 1996.

Arlt Roberto, *Mad Toy*, Duke University Press, 2002 ; *The Seven Madmen*, David R. Godine, 1984 ; *Los lanzallamas*, Barcelona, Bruguera, 1980.

Arciniegas German, *Le Chevalier d'Eldorado*, Paris, Espaces 34, 1995 ; *America Magica*, Buenos Aires, Sudamericana, 1961, 2 vols ; *El Continente de siete colores.*

Arguedas Jose Maria.

Asturias Miguel Ángel, *The President*, Wareland Press, 1997, *The Mirror of Lida sal: Tales Based On Mayan Myths And Guatemalan Legends, Latin America Literary Review Press,* 1997.

Ayala Francisco, *Morts de chiens* 1958

Bolivar Simon, *Obras completas*, Havana, Ed. de Vicente Lacuna, Lex, 1850, 3 vols.

Borges Jorge Luis, *Obras Completas*, Buenos Aires, Emece, 1974.

Cabrera Infante Guillermo, *Tres Tristes Tigres*, Barcelona, Ed. Six Barral, 1969. *Holy Smoke*, London, Ed. Faber and Faber, 1986. *Mea Cuba*, Barcelona, Ed. Plaza y Janes, 1992.

Carpentier Alejo, *Obras Completas*, Mexico, Siglo XXI, 1986, 9 vols : *La ciudad de las columnas*, Barcelona, Ed. Bruguera, 1982.

Cendrars Blaise, *Histoires vraies : en transatlantique dans la forêt vierge*, Paris, Grasset, 1936.

Cortazar Julio *in* Alcidia d'AMICO, *Buenos Aires Buenos Aires*, Buenos Aires, Sudamericana, 1968.

Dario Ruben, *Stories And Poems*, Dover Publications, 2002.

Ferrer Horacio, *El libro del tango*, Buenos Aires, Galerna, 1977.

Ferreira de Castro, *Forêt vierge*, Paris, Grasset, 1938.

Fuentes Carlos, *Agua Quemada*, Mexico, FCE, coll. « Tierra Firme », 1981.

Gallegos Romulo, *Doña Barbara*, Paris, Gallimard, 1951.

Garcia Marquez Gabriel, *The General in His Labyrinth*, New York, Penguin USA, 1991 ; *The Autumn Of The Patriarch*, New York, Harper Perennial, 1999.

Gomez de la Serna Ramon, *Explicación de Buenos Aires*, Buenos Aires*,* Ed. de la Flor, 1975.

Gheerbrandt Alain, *The Amazon: Past, Present And Future*, New York, Harry N. Abrams, 1992.

Guevara Ernesto Che, *The Bolivian Diary Of Ernesto Che Guevara*, Pathfinder Press, 1994.

Guillen Nicolas, *Le Chant de Cuba*, Paris, Belfond, 1984.

Güiraldes Ricardo, *Don Segundo Sombra*, University of Pittsburg, 1995.

Hernandez José, *Martin Fierro*, Universe.com, 1999.

Guzman Martin Luis, *L'Ombre du Caudillo*, Paris, Gallimard, 1997.

Kahlo Frida, *The Diary of Frida Kahlo,* New York, Abradale Press, 1998.

Marechal Léopoldo, *Adan Buenosayres*, Paris, Grasset, 1995.

Martí José, *Selecting Writings*, New York, Penguin USA, 2002.

Michaux Henri, *Ecuador: A Travel Journal*, Marlboro Press, 2001.

Naudin Jean Baptiste, *Hemingway à Cuba*, Paris, Le Chêne, 1997.

Neruda Pablo, *Chant Général*, Paris, Gallimard, 1977.

Paz Octavio, *The Labyrinth of Solitude*, Grove Press, 1985.

Roa Bastos Augusto, *I, The Supreme*, Dalkey Archive Pr., 2000.

Rulfo Juan, *The Burning Plain And Others Stories*, University Of Texas Press, 1971.

Sabato Ernesto, *Héros et tombes*, Paris, Seuil, coll. « Points », 1996.

Scalabrini Ortiz Raul, *Un homme seul et qui attend*

Supervielle Jules, *L'homme de la Pampa*, Paris, Gallimard, 1951.

Photography credits

p 4/5: ©Raul Benegas; p 9: ©Roland Paiva; p 10: ©British Library/AKG, Paris; p 11: ©National Library of France, Paris; p 12 top: ©Dagli Orti, Paris; p 12 bottom: ©AKG, Paris; p 13: ©AKG, Paris; p 14: ©Laziz Hamani; p 15: ©AKG, Paris; p 19: ©J. P. Barbier; p 20: ©Mexico, National Museum of History; p 21: ©Assouline; p 22 top: ©AKG, Paris; p 22 bottom: ©Laziz Hamani; p 23 top: ©Copenhagen, Royal Library; p 23b: ©AKG, Paris; p 24/25: ©Assouline; p 27: ©AKG, Paris; p 28 top: ©Dagli Orti, Paris; p 28 bottom: ©Sebastiao Salgado/Contact Press Images; p 29: ©Javier Ferrand; p 30: ©Michel Roget; p 31: ©Sagnoni/Rapho; p 32: ©Dagli Orti, Paris; p 33 top: ©Dagli Orti, Paris; p 34/35: ©Dagli Orti, Paris; p 38: ©Assouline; p 39: ©Aline Coquelle; p 42 top: ©Dagli Orti, Paris; p 42 bottom: ©Javier Ferrand; p 43: ©Javier Ferrand; p 44: ©Javier Ferrand; p 46: ©Javier Ferrand; p 47: ©Dagli Orti, Paris; p 48: ©Anne Menke; p 49: ©Pascaline David; p 50/51: ©Michel Roget; p 52: ©Michel Roget; P 53: ©Sergio Larrain/Magnum, Paris; p 54/55: ©Roland Paiva; p 56 top: ©Laziz Hamani; p 56 bottom: ©Raul Benegas; p 57: ©Raul Benegas; p 58/59: ©Kadir Van Lohuizen/Vu, Paris; p 60: ©Laziz Hamani; p 61: ©René Burri/Magnum, Paris; p 62: ©Laziz Hamani; p 63: ©René Burri/Magnum, Paris; p 64: ©Laziz Hamani; p 65 top: ©Laziz Hamani; p 65 bottom: ©Georges Gester/Rapho, Paris; p 66: ©Assouline; p 67: ©H. W. Silvester/Rapho, Paris; p 68: ©Nicolas Reynard; p 69: ©Nicolas Reynard; p 70: ©Nicolas Reynard; p 71: ©Nicolas Reynard; p 73: ©Nicolas Reynard; p 74: ©Sebastiao Salgado/Contact Press Images; p 75: ©Nicolas Reynard; p 76: ©Bridgeman Giraudon; p 79: ©Pedro Violle; p 80: ©Aline Coquelle; p 81: ©Thomas Hopker/Magnum, Paris; p 82/83: ©René Burri/Magnum, Paris; p 84: ©R. G. Ojeda/RMN, Paris; p 85: ©Assouline; p 87: ©Assouline; p 88 top: ©Patrick Jantet; p 88 bottom: ©Gilles Peress/Magnum, Paris; p 89: ©Patrick Jantet; p 90: ©Assouline; p 91: ©Patrick Jantet; p 94: ©Laziz Hamani; p 95: ©Laziz Hamani; p 96: ©Assouline; p 97: ©Laziz Hamani; p 98:© Iturbide/Vu, Paris; p 99: ©Laziz Hamani; p 100/101: ©Deborah Turbeville; p 102: ©Laziz Hamani; p 103 bottom: ©Laziz Hamani; p 104: ©Laziz Hamani; p 105: ©Laziz Hamani; p 106: ©Laziz Hamani; p 107: ©AKG, Paris; p 108/109: ©Deborah Turbeville; p 110: ©Christopher Rennie/Robert Harding Picture Library, London; p 111: ©Assouline; p 112: ©Deborah Turbeville ; p113 top: ©Dagli Orti, Paris; p 115: ©Pedro Violle; p 116: ©Pedro Violle; p 118/119: ©M. Yampolsky; p 121: ©Pedro Violle; p 122: ©Aline Coquelle; p 123: ©Zefa/Hoa Qui, Paris; p 125: ©Y. Lambert/Vu, Paris; p 126/127: ©D. A. Harvey/Magnum, Paris; p 129: ©Raul Benegas; p 130: ©BIFI; p 131: ©C. Pillitz/Rapho, Paris; p 132/133: ©C. Pillitz/Rapho, Paris ; p 135: ©Muñoz/Vu, Paris; p 136: ©Muñoz/Vu, Paris; p 137: ©Muñoz/Vu, Paris; p 138 top: ©Raul Benegas; p 138 bottom: ©Cinéplus; p 140: ©A. Groisman/Contact Press Images; p 141: ©N. Petotot/Hoa Qui, Paris; p 143: ©Raul Benegas; p 145: ©S. Torionne/Hémisphères, Paris; p 146: ©F. Ancellet/Rapho, Paris; p 147: ©Foto Blitz/Stills, Vanves; p 148/149: ©Patrick Jantet; p 150: ©K. Jarecke/Contact Press Images; p 153: ©Benoît Gysembergh; p 154: ©Illustration/Keystone, Paris; p 155: ©F.Scianna/Magnum, Paris; p 157: ©Bridgeman Giraudon; p 158: ©private collection; p 159: ©R. Depardon/Magnum, Paris; p 161: ©MOMA, New York;

Philippa